TAMING THE WILD Text

Literacy Strategies for Today's Reader

? Reading Critically

🔍 Reading Closely

💬 Reading Socially

🌐 Reading Widely

 Reading Deeply

Author

Pam Allyn, M.A. and Monica Burns, Ed.D.

Publishing Credits

Corinne Burton, M.A.Ed., *President*; Conni Medina, M.A.Ed., *Managing Editor*; Nika Fabienke, Ed.D., *Content Director*; Kat Bernardo, M.Ed., *Editor*; Shaun Bernadou, *Art Director*

Image Credits

p. 7 Gabe Gordon; p. 9 (girl) North Harnett Primary School; p. 9 (boy) Martha Munger; p. 102 Jenny Lewis; p. 110 LitWorld; p. 116 LitWorld; p. 123 Jenny Lewis; All other images © iStock and/or Shutterstock

Shell Education

5301 Oceanus Drive
Huntington Beach, CA 92649-1030
http://www.tcmpub.com/shell-education
ISBN 978-1-4258-1696-4
© 2018 Shell Educational Publishing, Inc.

Table of Contents

Acknowledgments

Crafting a book to combine our love of reading with the thoughtful integration of technology has been a collaborative process—both online and offline. Many thanks to our wonderful and wise editor, Kat Bernardo, for her guidance, insights, and enthusiasm. We share our gratitude for the insightful and caring work Nika Fabienke has done to help create such a beautiful outcome. The LitLife team, Linda Gallant, David Wilcox, Erica Freedman, Talia Kovas, and Laure Kohne, have added valuable knowledge and support to this work.

For their contribution of beautiful images of students taming the wild text, we would like to thank Lisa Williams, Emily McNeil, and the wonderful students of North Harnett Primary School. Thank you to Debbie Lera and her daughter Jada for their magical contributions. With thanks to Gabriel Gordon for his magnificent drawing of the "TWT Child."

A special note of appreciation to Rich Levitt, Sara Johnson, and Emily Smith of Teacher Created Materials for helping *Taming the Wild Text* come to fruition.

Introduction

Why Reading Feels Different Now

It is a new era for reading. Though the child in bed with a flashlight may seem like a quaint image from the past, the idea of illuminated reading under the covers can be as true today as it was yesterday. Today's child can become immersed in the world of reading, but the light of the story glowing in the late corners of the evening may come from a screen rather than a flashlight. The reader of today is reading but not always one book at a time. This reader is athletic: jumping from idea to idea, genre to genre. He or she is reading across many platforms, many types of text, from visual to print, from moving images to primary source photographs. However, the child with the flashlight is still within us and within our children. The print book is not gone, and the technology has not taken over. Rather, the world is becoming a truly blended one. Reading is a lasting innovation in many forms. It sustains us, guides us, and makes us whole.

Many books have proposed that reading on paper is out of style, that adults are the "digital immigrants" and students are the "digital natives," that teachers and parents have to catch up to them, and that the only way kids will keep reading is if they are flooded with tablets and other technologies in classrooms.

But just when many thought the end of print was near, in 2016, sales of children's books exceeded sales of adult books. Overall, sales of print books are climbing, and new independent bookstores are opening at a relatively steady clip. The American Booksellers Association (ABA) reported that 60 independent bookstores opened in 31 states and the District of Columbia in 2015, besting 2016's total by one. And so, in the midst of the new era, readers are becoming more comfortable using many platforms, and students are growing up in a world that will have more options than ever. So it is not an "either/or" world of reading; it is a world of open possibility for countless kinds of reading to exist for children. Teachers and parents must strive to develop children who can tame the wild text anywhere, in any form.

What Readers Need

Reading has become wilder than ever. The world now is full of many types of text emerging through new technologies. Grammar is changing, devices are changing—even fonts are changing and evolving. It is a very exciting time to be a reader. But a reader's needs, like that child under the covers with the flashlight, don't change that much. All readers need are:

- A choice in the text that they read
- Access to a wide variety of texts
- Time to read (and time specifically to peruse and choose what they read)
- Mentor readers who guide and inspire them
- An environment in which it feels safe to take risks
- Affirmative feedback regarding reading progress
- The opportunity to have an ever-changing identity as a reader (I am the kind of reader who…)
- A community of supportive and encouraging fellow readers

This book highlights key ways in which teachers can tame the wildness of all the texts children are reading. By providing structures and strategies that support the growing reader, teachers can launch their students into the world of 21st century reading.

This book is about teaching students to read on every platform and in every genre, to struggle with text, to break through to new ideas when reading text, and to become the kind of fearless reader who tames the wild text.

Independent Reading Tips

When classroom libraries are organized with books categorized in meaningful ways, students begin to connect themes and find similar structures among texts. Whether using book baskets or e-reader "shelves," you can help students make these connections by grouping books in engaging and exciting ways. For example, a survival-themed basket would contain fiction titles such as *Sign of the Beaver*, *Nature Girl*, and *Number the Stars* as well as informational text such as *Survival Kid: A Practical Guide to Wilderness Survival*. Storm-safety pamphlets, *Backpacker* or *National Geographic Kids* magazines, and articles from news sources would make great additions to this category as well. These engaging grouping techniques are more likely to pique the interest of a reader than a category simply titled "Lois Lowry" or "Gary Paulsen."

Features of This Book

This book is designed to help teachers help students tame the wild text, wherever they find it, from the print book they read in their science class to the online world of news. It is not specific to one device or one particular classroom setup. The big ideas and actionable lessons can be tailored to different grade levels, different types of devices, and different technology plans. Although some may feel like a one-to-one environment, where each student has a tablet or laptop in their hands is ideal, there is so much that can be done with just a few tablets or a weekly visit to the computer lab.

Key features embedded throughout the next chapters are designed to help support students as they tame the wild text. Callout boxes feature lesson ideas with steps to putting these ideas into action. Teachers are encouraged to read through these activities and individualize them, connecting learning goals and teaching style. Many activities have graphic organizers that can be reproduced for students or used as inspiration to scaffold instruction. A full-sized version of each of these reproducible sheets can be found in Appendix C on pages 155–175. Over the course of this book, teachers will have access to recommendations for websites, mobile applications, books, and text sets that match each of the Five Habits for Reading that are introduced in this book. Each time you see the icon of a hand holding a smartphone®, you will know that the accompanying information has been included in Appendix D on pages 176–181.

Throughout this book, you'll see references to the wonderful work that LitWorld is doing around the globe. Pam Allyn founded LitWorld in 2007 to bring a broader, more transformational approach to how literacy is shared and used by children in all its forms. In 2013, Monica joined the team as the edtech specialist, with a goal of inspiring communities across the world to be their own best literacy incubators. Pam, Monica, and the rest of the LitWorld team help communities identify and use all of their available resources—from children's own stories, to technologies, to books in hand—making sure every child in the community gets a chance to read.

LitWorld
Be the Story.

This book is really for all of the people who surround a child's life with the opportunity to read. For this reason, a shareable letter, in both English and Spanish, has been included at the end of every chapter. This will help parents, caregivers, and teachers work together to develop a child who is unafraid to tackle the texts of the world.

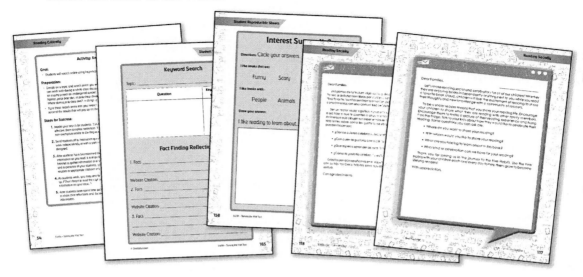

In order to tame the wild text in the new era, students must develop five habits for Reading. Students who read widely, critically, deeply, closely, and socially will be ready to tackle texts across all genres and platforms. Welcome to a journey that will transform teaching and learning in today's classrooms!

Introducing the Five Habits for Reading

Chapter 1: Reading Widely

Students of all ages should interact with a range of text. Teachers must inspire this generation of readers to become voracious consumers of language and to strike a balance between literature and informational text in order to achieve an understanding of text structure in the new era. These readers leapfrog between genres, platforms, pages, and screens with the dexterity and fearlessness of pole-vaulters. It is both a privilege and a responsibility to be born during a time when literacy instruction in school and beyond requires such cognitive athleticism, but students are up to the challenge. This chapter presents strategies for introducing new text types, from infographics to social media posts, in addition to honoring favorite traditional texts.

Chapter 2: Reading Critically

Successful students think critically about what they read. Never has this been more important than in a world where anyone can instantly publish their writing online. In this chapter, readers find lesson ideas and activities that help students evaluate text and question the accuracy and authenticity of the materials in front of them. Reading critically means having opinions and taking a stance on one's reading perspective. This chapter gives online and off-line tips for how to help students really activate their minds for critical thinking.

Chater 3: Reading Deeply

Everyone has had the feeling of getting lost in a book, reading deeply and attentively, all while exploring new stories and falling in love with the characters. Students should be able to respond to their reading, share their feelings about a book, and think beyond the text. Reading deeply means immersing oneself in the magic of the reading experience, asking questions, and delighting in the findings while reading between the lines. This chapter helps teachers guide students in that direction, reading for pleasure, and reading for the pursuit of greater understandings not only in the text but also in oneself. This chapter includes lessons that highlight the many ways technology can energize traditional reading activities and honor student passions.

Chapter 4: Reading Closely

Close reading is a joyful experience of attending to text, conversing about author choices, and discussing a reading with text in hand while perusing the contents. Students need to support their thinking about a text with evidence by reading literature and informational text closely. In this chapter, readers learn how technology tools can help build background knowledge and alter traditional interactions with text. Protocols for close reading on any platform are shared, as are ways to help students exercise and flex their reading muscles one sentence or phrase at a time.

Chapter 5: Reading Socially

Reading socially means that students are reading in order to be a part of a community. They may want to share new knowledge with a classmate or travel with a friend through a fantasy novel. Both teachers and students should see their work as readers and reading instructors as a social activity. This chapter explains how to use technology tools to connect with authentic audiences and set a purpose for reading socially.

Chapter 6: Assessment in the New Era

In this chapter, readers have access to helpful rubrics for the Five Habits. These can be used to track students' progress and to inspire one-to-one and small group work. Readers also learn about the amazing ways in which technology is fueling the power to really know and understand students. Here, readers receive new tech solutions for how to follow students as they learn and grow as readers. Formative and performance-based assessments are addressed in this chapter as two valuable ways to see students evolve throughout the school year: no surprises at the end! Minute by minute, day by day, students flourish and grow. This chapter helps teachers track students' progress and use that data to inform instruction.

Chapter 7: Next Steps

In order to help teachers jump right into the work of taming the wild text, this chapter provides easy-to-follow action steps. From working alongside colleagues to learning more about today's technology, there are immediate things teachers can do to make the transitions to the new era feel comfortable and exciting. These action steps should provide readers with an easy-to-follow way to bring this book to life!

A Note for Teachers

In *Taming the Wild Text*, we'll explore the Five Habits of readers in the digital age and bring them together to paint a picture of a full reading life. Whether reading a paperback or on an e-book reader, the practical tips and techniques woven into our discussion of digital and print reading experiences can serve as inspiration for the entire school year. We hope that you will jot down notes in the margin, add a sticky note to a page, or highlight a favorite passage. We encourage you to bring this book to professional learning communities or your grade-level team. Read it together, try out lesson ideas in partners, and strategize ways to connect students' interests and passions with their needs in the digital age.

Beyond the walls of the classroom, after the school day ends, parents and caregivers are essential components of the reading lives of our students. They anchor the work that happens in classroom by demonstrating their own reading lives, sharing reading time with their children, and building their understanding of what reading looks like when students have devices in their hands. At the end of each chapter, you'll find a letter that we've written for families. You can read this book alongside your students' parents or send home these notes to foster a home/school conversation around how we can help our children tame the wild text together.

A Note for Caregivers

We are so excited to have you along on this reading journey! Your support in balancing print and digital text is an essential piece of the puzzle for growing strong readers. This book was designed to provide an overview of big ideas in literacy instruction as well as a window into the world of thoughtful use of technology integration. There is information within these pages that can help you as you support your children outside school hours.

Digging into this text with a reading partner can elevate your reading experience. The PTA at your school may have a monthly or quarterly book club to discuss innovations in education where *Taming the Wild Text* can provide a framework for your conversations. A school-sponsored event or an afternoon spent sharing favorite reading apps can introduce fellow parents to the ways digital text is changing the world.

We hope this book will inspire you to think about the reading experiences you engage in with your children. From celebrating a range of genres, introducing children to your own favorite books (now available on a tablet), or trying out a virtual-reality experience for the first time, you have the power to inspire your children.

One of our favorite stories to share in this vein comes from a parent. While she and her child were reading a book together, they came across the word *plains*, a word the mother was sure her daughter didn't know. Instead of simply telling her the meaning of the word, they went to YouTube on their tablet to watch a video together. Her daughter had a clear picture of the setting of the book thanks to a few simple clicks on their screen. We hope you are inspired to use technology with your family of readers, too!

A Note for Administrators

We invite you to use this book as a catalyst for connection between the teachers and administrative teams in your school or district. It will take all of you working together to prepare your students for reading in the 21st century. Your teachers may feel overwhelmed by the many different platforms of reading in which your students are engaged. They may feel overwhelmed by the "either/or" nature of the conversation around literacy up to this point. But this book is designed to relieve some of those tensions.

Please consider using this book in the following ways:

- Read one chapter at a time over the course of consecutive faculty meetings.
- Read one chapter at a time over the course of a parent/teacher study group.
- Pull out activities to try as a whole faculty, and then report success and challenge across grade levels.
- Assign chapters to a specific group of teachers across grade levels and then invite them to present their reflections to the larger faculty group.

And as for you, we invite you to become an instructional leader in mobilizing your school community. Use the Five Habits as a call to action in your districtwide strategy plan. Encourage your teachers to mark progress and success through the Five Habits rather than just through an end-of-year test score. In your addresses to the faculty, challenge them to embrace the struggle, the newness of the reading experience in this new era. Finally, take time to savor the successes as you work together with teachers, parents, and students.

Reading Widely

Pablo, a third-grader, explores his passion for tigers in the first 10 minutes of his independent reading time and then skips over to his tablet to see real photos of them in the wild. In the second 10 minutes, he enjoys a joke book with his friend, and then they compile their own jokes in Google Docs™. In the final 10 minutes of independent reading, Pablo makes a list on his tablet of the books he needs from the library for his social studies project. This is reading widely.

First-grader Kareem moves effortlessly from a picture book with magical bears to an informational text on butterflies. Fifth-grader Jessica can shift her thinking from a current-events article on her tablet to a favorite chapter book. These students have the skills that help them dive into a sea of reading and make their way through uncharted waters. They understand how to read widely as they work to tame the wild text.

The ability to read across genres for a variety of purposes is a characteristic of strong, independent learners. Although most students have favorite books, authors, and genres, it's essential for young readers to develop skills that allow them to explore a wide variety of genres. Strong readers should be able to move from an informational text in the morning to a classic piece of literature in the afternoon, changing their purpose for reading over the course of the day. Reading widely includes an understanding and appreciation of what different types of texts have to offer.

For English language learners, reading widely poses both an opportunity and a challenge. Discovering new genres is exciting, but the reader must also get the "trick" of the text: how does this text "go"? English language learners are potentially overwhelmed by the decoding and comprehension work they're doing, and so the switch in genre may be problematic for them. On the other hand, there is an opportunity here. For the English language learner, reading a fictional text set during the civil rights movement may be very challenging with new vocabulary and character names. But when that text is paired with a nonfiction text on the same subject, the English language learner is able to break through some of the hard parts of reading with help from the photos, graphs, and charts that provide visual supports.

For below-level learners, there are often times when, because of the ways students have been identified as "struggling," they miss some of the dynamic energy of the wide reading that other students in the same class can enjoy. Their intervention time includes specific texts designed to instruct. But below level learners benefit so greatly from abundant opportunities to read widely. Provide struggling readers with time to explore a variety of text with their peers. They should not be spending all of their time decoding texts or even doing comprehension strategy work. Reading widely means they are browsing, scanning, skimming, enjoying, viewing pictures, not finishing a book, or skipping to something new. Let below level learners be as much a part of this as their peers. It will make a world of difference.

Accessing Texts of Many Genres

Students who read widely interact with a range of genres. From narrative nonfiction to fantasy, they are consistently engaging with a wide variety of texts. When children read across genres, they are exposed to stories and information from all walks of life. They begin to experience the world from different points of view while learning about new topics and discovering answers to their questions.

The shift from a classroom library of picture books to an ample supply of diverse texts demonstrates the value of preparing students to read widely. Children in kindergarten can distinguish among genres in simple forms. Older students can explore the characteristics of genres in more detailed forms as they categorize different types of fiction, nonfiction, and poetry. Although units of study taught during a school year may focus on a specific genre, make it a point to highlight student favorites across genres and subgenres to encourage independent readers to read widely.

Cultural Representation

Classroom texts should reflect ideas that represent the classroom, the community, and the world; building this type of library is a chance to create an equal opportunity vehicle that contains interests for all. The collection should be both worldly and intimate. A broad range of texts invites students to become citizens of the world as they travel to faraway places and climb into the lives of people unlike themselves. A broad classroom collection sends a clear message that a world of discovery is awaiting students, while a limited collection sends the opposite message. In short, access to well-curated resources is nothing less than a students'-rights issue.

Examples of Genres

Fiction

- fantasy
- historical fiction
- science fiction
- fairy tale
- myth
- fable
- folktale
- mystery
- realistic fiction
- graphic novel
- short story

Nonfiction

- memoir
- news article
- reference book
- textbook
- encyclopedia
- biography
- autobiography
- essay
- report
- blog
- journal article
- informative picture books
- infographic
- functional text
- scientific text
- mathematical text
- website
- historical text
- map

Poetry

- haiku
- sonnet
- cinquain
- blank verse
- free verse
- spoken word
- rap

Argument/Opinion

- editorial
- review/recommendation: product, music, film, book, etc.
- blog
- social media post
- letter to the editor
- advertisement
- public service announcement

Rudine Sims Bishop distills the rights issues in the most eloquent terms. Bishop (1990) described the ways in which literature can serve as windows, sliding glass doors, and mirrors. Books can become windows, offering a "view of worlds that may be real or imagined, familiar or strange." Readers can then treat these windows as sliding glass doors by walking through them and into the world created by the author. These same windows can also serve as mirrors, reflecting the readers' lives and experiences back to them "as part of the larger human experience." Literature, particularly multicultural literature, can provide both self-affirmation and a way to learn about and appreciate various cultures, dialects, and ways of being in the world. Literature has the power to teach about and honor readers' differences and similarities.

mirror

window

reminds me
of myself

different-
see and learn
new things

_____ is like a mirror
to me because_____.

It's encouraging to see a significant improvement in the number of books representing different cultures. A 2015 study by the Children's Book Center at the University of Wisconsin showed more diversity presented in trade books published in the United States. However, educators still have miles to go before all children can find a mirror in their classroom libraries.

Whether at home or in the classroom, prioritize the mirrors-and-windows library, the mirrors-and-windows world, the mirrors-and-windows conversations. Every child deserves an opportunity for self-discovery while peering out into the larger world.

Cross-Curricular Connections

National expectations for literacy encourage incorporating informational text into every aspect of the curriculum, starting in kindergarten: "A variety of studies suggest young children can interact successfully with informational text when given the opportunity to do so" (Duke 2003). The implications of this shift are vast; the very texture of the classroom reading collection will take on a fresh look and a new purpose, and the ELA texts on hand will be enriched by more media-based and modern informational sources.

As teachers develop essential questions that align with reading goals, they must pause to evaluate goals in content-area instruction.

> *"Can you connect your lesson on key details to a reading passage on the rock cycle during a science lesson? Can you guide students in a word-choice close reading of a primary source document in a social studies lesson?"*

Making cross-curricular connections is more than killing two birds with one stone. Connecting content in multiple subject areas helps students see an application for reading skills outside a chapter book or a read-aloud. The texts used in a reading lesson could be based on content area goals in social studies and science. For example, a book like *A Train to Somewhere* by Eve Bunting could be used to teach a reading strategy during a Social Studies unit on Westward Expansion. Teachers should examine curriculum maps for social studies and science when choosing texts to share with students. These lessons and activities show students that reading does not have to be experienced in isolation but can open doors to new learning.

Interest Surveys

Interest surveys give a glimpse into student thinking and can help identify texts, topics, and themes that will grab their attention. An interest survey may take place during the first week of school to help a teacher determine how to best organize her classroom library. Student interests change over the course of the year, and periodic interest surveys can aid a teacher on her quest to provide students with new books that will grab—and hold—their attention.

Digital Options for Interest Surveys:

- Google Form
- Socrative
- Kahoot

For the youngest of students, interest surveys can be as simple as having students color a smiley face on a page or tap a screen of pictures to show what they like to learn about. Older students may respond to an open-ended question and list their favorite authors and genres. Interest surveys provide children with a voice. A teacher's genuine interest in learning about the passions of her students becomes evident when she honors the choices of the children in the classroom.

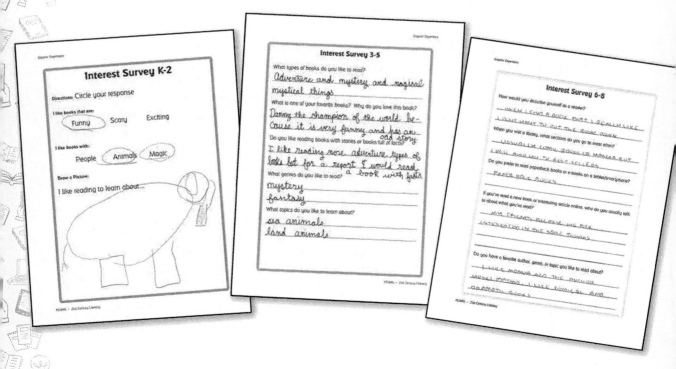

Digital Genres

Readers today have access to an endless amount of content. Students who read widely can cultivate the tools necessary for making meaning of digital genres. The readers of digital text must be critical thinkers who can skim, digest, and learn while adding in an extra layer of evaluation.

21st Century Reading Tip

When sharing blog posts with students, be mindful of any advertisements, pop-ups, or links embedded in the text, and remind students how you expect them to navigate the page.

This section examines these new digital genres to define their meaning and explain their significance. Incorporating these text types into instruction is a must in 21st century classrooms. An understanding of how to tame the wild text and navigate new text types is an essential component of college and career readiness.

Blog Posts

A blog post is a special kind of website that features content posted in chronological order. A single blog post can range in length from a few hundred to a few thousand words. Many blogs have one focus, such as a collection of posts featuring favorite recipes or fitness tips. Other blogs feature posts on a range of topics, usually posted by one person or a single organization.

Just like traditional print texts, there are common features to blog posts found on different websites. Every blog post has a title, an author, and a body of text. Most include an image and subheadings to organize the information in the post. Most blogs contain links to take the reader to more information about a topic. These links could connect to other content on that particular website or to information published somewhere else on the Internet. One unique feature of blogs is that they often have a comments section at the bottom of the page. These comments give readers an opportunity to share their opinions and ask the author questions while also viewing and analyzing the opinions of other readers.

Activity: Reading a Blog Post

Goals:

- Make connections to what children have accomplished as readers.

- Acknowledge the differences in digital text.

- Show students how to use a blog to share content on a topic.

- Discuss author bias or media literacy.

Preparation:

- Decide ahead of time what type of blog post features you plan on sharing with students. If you decide to share a blog post that is printed on paper, the experience will be different from a blog post in which students interact with a digital tool.

- Decide on the blog features you want to highlight with students, such as: author bio, hyperlinks, or the comments section. Choose a blog post that contains these features.

Procedure:

- Display the blog post so that all students can see the page by projecting it on the board or having a copy in front of each student.

- Before reading the text aloud to your class, have them scroll or skim through the page. Ask students to share with a partner some of the things they notice about the blog post, such as the way the text is organized or special features they see. Bring the class back together and highlight some of the important features that make a blog post similar to or different from other pieces of text that students have explored.

- Share with students that the purpose of a blog is for someone to post updates about their life, how they feel about an issue, or to give information on a topic, and that most blogs have a specific focus.

- Ask students to read the blog post you have picked with a partner. You may guide them with specific focus questions, such as *What have we already learned about this topic? Who is the author, and why did he or she write this post?* or *Where else can I go to get more information on this topic?*

Feature Articles

Students who read widely are able to gather information, learn about a special event or notable person, and explore new worlds through feature articles. Feature articles can be found in print magazines and online publications. Many favorite print publications also have an online presence, so you can find articles by searching their website. There are also several online-only resources for feature articles that give teachers and students easy access to quality content.

When introducing feature articles to students, teachers should discuss text features and author bias in the same way they would address these topics in print text. As feature articles often examine historical or scientific topics, they can be used to complement social studies or science units of study.

Resources for Kid-Friendly Feature Articles

- Newsela
- News-O-Matic
- Smithsonian Tween Tribune
- TIME For Kids

Reading "Short"

Readers in the 21st century need to navigate digital genres of all forms. Social media platforms feature concise messages and require a special set of reading skills. Students who are scrolling through short text must understand how to read between the lines and search for meaning behind just a sentence or two. This medium offers ample opportunity to practice critical thinking skills.

One medium for short-text mentors is Twitter®. Twitter limits writers to 140 characters, so posts must be concise and to the point. Readers of a tweet have only a sentence or two to digest. Students can analyze a deceptively simple tweet for author's purpose, bias, and text-to-world connections with the same level of effort as a close read of a passage from a piece of classic literature.

The action of reading short helps students to think beyond the seemingly simple characters or a single sentence in a book.

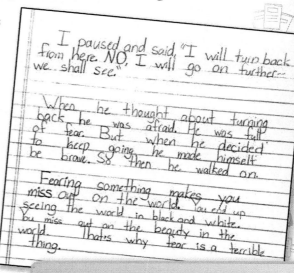

Lifting a Line (see page 26)

Activity: Lifting a Line

Goals:

- Students will identify a short line that moves them, surprises them, or makes them wonder.

Procedure:

- Ask students to put a star next to a line that:
  - Jumps out at them
  - Makes them wonder
  - Shocks them
  - Makes them want to cry
  - Makes them think differently
  - Makes them want to laugh
  - Makes them want to talk to someone

- Invite them to "lift that line" and write it at the top of the screen or page. Then, have students reflect and write for two minutes. Use that thinking to explore what kind of talking and reading may come next. For example, in "The Wood Pile" by Robert Frost, one student selects the line: ". . .I will turn back from here. / No, I will go farther—and we shall see." Inspired by this line, the student reflects on the author's purpose as well as how the words act as a mirror, allowing her to look inward at herself (See page 25).

- After the initial reflection, challenge students to read widely, connecting this text with others. Students could:

  - Read the news and discuss how this line resonates.

  - Read another poem written later by Frost and see if his thoughts on the quirks of human nature change.

  - Read a poem written by a classmate and see if there are common themes.

  - Students can also lift a line from a text and locate an image that connects to the mood or tone of the selection. Graphic design and poster-making tools make it easy to layer text on top of an image. Some of our favorites are Spark Post (web, iOS), Canva (web, iOS) and PicCollage (iPad).

Readers must read between the lines. Teachers and students can converse about context and word choice while unpacking lines lifted from a text. Whether this analysis takes place with a tweet from a notable writer or an excerpt from a favorite book, reading short is a skill that students need when interacting with traditional and digital text. Students can find much to discuss in a quote, such as this example from *Pride and Prejudice*: "Vanity and pride are different things, though the words are often used synonymously."

Balancing the Genres

As teachers prepare students for the rigors of real-world reading, there is an expectation that today's English language arts classrooms blend instruction of fiction with informational and persuasive texts. This balance builds on young children's natural curiosity about the world, supports their vocabulary development and word knowledge in organic ways, and works to develop their growing concepts of reading and writing. Considering the fact that around 90 percent of daily reading outside school falls under the category of informational text, incorporating focused study of these genres into lesson set objectives begins to sound not only beneficial but also necessary.

Some great ways to balance the use of literature and informational text:

- Make sure weekly read alouds include examples that represent the variety of the genre. Traditionally, teachers tend to gravitate toward fiction for read alouds, but blog posts, a nonfiction retelling of a baseball game, or a news report can all be used. All may be examples of wonderful writing and can be riveting to students of all ages.

- Use text sets as features in the classroom library. Pair a book about lions with *The Lion and the Mouse* by Jerry Pinkney. Pair a nonfiction text about world cultures with *The Breadwinner* by Deborah Ellis. Search for an article hosted online by an organization like Newsela or Smithsonian Tween Tribune that connects to a theme in a favorite read-aloud book. If students are reading the realistic fiction book *Redwoods* by Jason Chin, teachers can introduce them to a news article on conservation initiatives in California.

- Have students match up a theme to texts across genres. Students choose a theme, and then others in the class add titles either to an online forum or to a bulletin board in the classroom.

- Add QR codes to literature books in the classroom library that connect students to a related piece of informational text. This QR code could link students to a short biography of the author or an online encyclopedia entry that shares information about a topic featured in the book.

Evolving Text Structures

Children who read widely should notice text structure and organization as they explore digital and print text. Active readers attend to patterns in a text, notice how text is presented, and gather information from this organization. Traditional lessons on text structure can be tailored to digital text, and digital text experiences can be leveraged to help children understand the organization of print text.

The term *text structure* refers to how a text is formed and built and the student's awareness of its grammar, punctuation, form, and style. Text structures also relate to the way words lay out on a page, which is different depending on genre. Nonfiction text will show more lists and unique uses of white space to feature charts and graphs. Narrative text tends to use imagery and painting in a more artistic manner, either in a picture book or as starters for chapters in novels. Text structures belong to each genre, and each genre is made dynamic by text structures. The student as a tamer of text is highly aware of what it means to read actively—to say, "I wonder what the author was doing here, and why." Students will notice that authors tend to repeat favorite text structures. They may vary sentence length or use grammar in interesting yet specific ways to highlight their style.

As readers, students breathe in the words and imagery that the author breathes out. In the midst of this give-and-take, students are tuned into the following types of thinking:

- How is this author using grammar to convey a point of view or a big idea?
- How is this author selecting a specific genre to help us best understand his or her theme or idea?
- What role do white space, punctuation, and word choice play in this sentence or paragraph?

Digital Text Structures

Teachers know that they must show students how to make their way through the structure of a print text and how to navigate digital pathways. Encourage students to think of this skill as a kind of X-ray vision that allows them to better understand the author's intent behind a piece of sophisticated writing. This superpower can even help them *anticipate* the next move an author will make based on the type of structure in place.

Text structure in digital text varies significantly in quality. Some digital text can feel like a substitution for print text—the only difference in reading behavior is how students consume the content. Other digital text provides a completely redefined reading experience in which students can tap on the screen to access a three-dimensional model or press a button for a virtual reality experience. Ruben Puentedura explains this idea of substitution vs. redefinition in the SAMR model. It is important to understand that the quality of digital texts will vary and therefore the ability to have an interactive experience with completely new text structures will vary as well.

SAMR Model

The SAMR model, developed by Ruben Puentedura, introduces a way in which educators can examine technology integration. Substitution, augmentation, modification, and redefinition are the four levels of the model. These levels indicate the depth of technology integration in different learning experiences. The SAMR model is often used by teachers to reflect on their use of technology in the classroom.

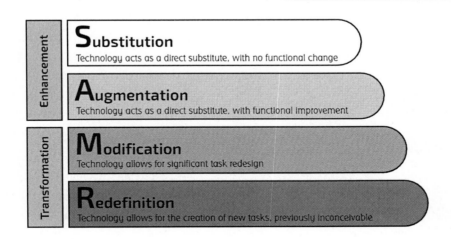

Enhancement

Substitution
Technology acts as a direct substitute, with no functional change

Augmentation
Technology acts as a direct substitute, with functional improvement

Transformation

Modification
Technology allows for significant task redesign

Redefinition
Technology allows for the creation of new tasks, previously inconceivable

One well established text structure sleuthing method to try out is to have students read similar information that is presented using different text structures. Scaffold this type of lesson by providing students with a comprehensive list or table of signal words associated with each type of text structure. (A helpful example can be found on the National Education Association's "Using Text Structure" web page: www.nea.org.) With these signal words in hand, students can build a repository of textual cues that will help them navigate the wilds of an expository text that may present a top-level structure of problem and solution and then begin to veer between comparison and sequence structures in order to explain why the planet is heating up. Consider utilizing interest survey results to help guide mentor text choices for students to review in order to become structure sleuths capable of understanding hybrid texts online and off-line.

In addition to the tried-and-true aid of using customized graphic organizers to analyze different types of text, students may benefit from using the SQRW method when tasked with making sense of digital expository texts rife with hybrid text structures and hyperlinks. Begin by surveying the passage (S), formulating a question (Q), reading for information (R), and finally writing down the results of the search (W) (Wolpert and Vacca-Rizopoulus 2012; Bos and Vaughn 2005). Using these notes as a foundation, model what it means to understand the value of a hyperlink. Make a judgment about the value, safety, and relevance of the link (Hodgson 2010). Ask students to be vigilant screeners of the sea of information at their fingertips and to refer back to the purpose set for reading at the beginning of the exercise. If they do decide to click on a link, ask them to chart their path from the original source in their notes, providing tangible evidence of the nonlinear structure found in the majority of online expository texts. The frequency of this type of exercise is key: when students take on the role of structure sleuths, they experience the power of having a plan.

Infographics

In a world of varied media, teachers must model for students how to gather information from the visuals they see on a web page: captions, diagrams, and the ever popular infographics.

Tools for Locating Infographics

Although a Google image search for *kid-friendly infographics* will turn up great results, you may want to check out these resources:

- Kids Discover
- *Infographics: Human Body* by Peter Grundy
- Reading Rocket's Infographic Board

Infographics provide a visual representation of information. Instead of reading a paragraph full of survey data, an infographic is a picture that shows the information. It is a snapshot that helps a reader comprehend numerical data. Just like a caption on a photograph, infographics provide essential information. Although infographics are printed in traditional reading materials like newspapers, this type of medium is especially common in blog posts and news articles published online. Since an infographic is a visual representation of data, it can be tweaked to place emphasis on a certain set of conclusions. The inherent bias in infographics make them important tools to use in a conversation on author bias.

Activity: Reading an Infographic

Goals:
- Teach students to linger on the caption underneath a photo, or pause to think about the relevance of a map or a graph.
- Guide students in making meaning of this digital media.

Preparation:
- Locate a handful of infographics that are appropriate in level for your readers. We have included one in Appendix C on page 160.
- Prepare a few noticings and questions before you lead the class lesson.

Procedure:
- Model how to notice the information that an infographic provides. Make sure to point out how you learned or wondered about a topic based on the information provided. You may pose questions like *What is the big idea of this infographic? What does the creator of this infographic want me to know? Why may an author include this infographic in his or her article? How else could the creator of this infographic represent this information?*
- Independently or in pairs, have students examine a new infographic, discussing and responding to the same questions you modeled. You may decide to have all students look at the same infographic or differentiate this task by having students look at leveled content.
- When students are finished, show them how to notice and analyze an infographic when it is embedded in an article.

Tools for Creating Infographics

- Keynote
- Canva
- Pages

Activity: Creating an Infographic

Goals:

- Create an infographic using authentic data.

Procedure:

- Have students collect a set of data around a topic (or provide a data set). They may want to create an infographic around a big idea, such as *What kind of books do students at our elementary school like to read?*, or they may want to gather information and create an infographic that connects to a topic they are reading about, such as *What do fourth graders think about global warming?*

- Once students have collected their data, show a handful of examples of what an infographic can look like. Depending on your group of students, you may want to provide a template for them to work with.

- Give students time to brainstorm images or icons they would like to include in their infographic. Talk about the way that color and fonts can convey a mood or set a tone.

- Working in pairs or individually, have students sketch out their ideas with pencil and paper. Then, introduce them to an online tool for creating infographics.

- Model how to use this tool to create an infographic in order to clarify the expectations, and explain how to use the tool in the context of this project.

- After students have finished, let them jigsaw into small groups to share their work. This conversation can include reflection and peer feedback.

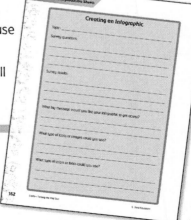

Digital or Print?

Research on Digital Text

Powerful research in the field of education clarifies the impact of digital text. Myriad studies examining the ways in which readers interact with the stories on screen provide a guide for thinking about digital text while navigating different ways to gather information and hear stories as readers. Cognitive neuroscientist Dr. Maryanne Wolf, an expert on the reading brain, is dedicated to this critical line of inquiry and is currently developing apps that will help students engage with digital text. She is aware that educators cannot afford to ignore the rich possibilities that lie within the realm of digital literacy.

Wolf is encouraged by a recent study that examined how a thoughtfully constructed digital annotation technique affected comprehension or the ability to "read deeply" among a group of fifth graders. After being taught how to use a collaborative reading annotation system, the digital experimental group "significantly outperformed" the paper-based annotation group in the areas of direct and explicit comprehension, inferential comprehension performance, and the use of reading strategies (Chen and Chen 2014). In her 2014 *New Yorker* article, "Being a Better Online Reader," psychologist and author Maria Konnikova cites Wolf as stating that "the same plasticity that allows us to form a reading circuit to begin with, and short-circuit the development of deep reading if we allow it, also allows us to learn how to duplicate deep reading in a new environment" (Konnikova 2014).

This "go to the mountain" approach to digital literacy is shared by other leading researchers in the field, such as Lisa Guernsey and Michael Levine, the authors of *Tap, Click, Read: Growing Readers in a World of Screens.* Guernsey and Levine advocate blending media and reading literacies so that all students may gain access to "Readialand," their playful term for "a place where reading and media are joined in service of each other and new literacy opportunities are accessible to all families" (Guernsey and Levine 2015). They make the crucial point that to downplay or even ignore the possibilities of technology in the classroom is to disenfranchise our most vulnerable students who may benefit from new content and teaching methods enhanced by technology as a means of narrowing the "digital divide." Their perspective is grounded in the demonstrated benefits of "joint media engagement," or JME, meaning that moments of engagement (e.g., dialogic questioning) between adults and children as young as infants increases learning potential when consuming both print and digital texts. Another study cited by Guernsey and Levine showed the advantages of children learning from "nonverbal multimedia features...that match the story text" in electronic storybooks (2015). In other words, the study saw children benefiting from exposure to *multimedia* (e.g., animations and visual effects, sound effects, background music) as opposed to *hypermedia* features such as games and "hotspots" irrelevant to the text (Bus, Takacs, and Kegel 2015). This distinction between how the children reacted to the multimedia and hypermedia features in digital narratives underscores how advances in technology can also advance literacy as long as they are "consistent with the way the human processing system works" (Bus, Takacs, and Kegel 2015). More intrusive elements have the potential to overload young readers and impede their progress toward a deeper understanding of the story at hand, a possibility worth the consideration of teachers and parents alike.

And though some studies suggests that narrative-reading experiences on electronic devices may complicate a student's sense of immersion in the text, many researchers agree that results are mixed and more research must be done before any definitive conclusions can be made.

Until then, teachers must thoughtfully consider the many exciting affordances of the digital technologies at their fingertips—including portability, built-in dictionaries, and customizable settings, just to name a few. These benefits must be weighed against the demonstrated perennial value of the printed page, and a customized learning experience must be crafted with the benefits and drawbacks of both mediums in mind.

Research on Print Text

It's important to understand the way that readers interact with the words on the page when looking closely at the differences between reading digital text and print text. There are technical terms like *haptic dissonance* (i.e., the conflict we feel when the act of reading an e-book challenges our expectations of how the physical or haptic act of reading a book should feel), used by some to explain why rumors of print's death have been so greatly exaggerated. Others, like Abigail Sellen, a principal researcher at Microsoft Research Cambridge, suggest that readers don't feel the same sense of ownership of an e-book as they do with a print book because the act of reading the former isn't accompanied by the tangible expectations that come with reading the latter, e.g., feeling the pleasant friction of the page's fibers, flipping through pages to quickly reference a favorite passage, or feeling the weight of the book like another presence in the room. Sellen says, "They [readers] think of using an e-book, not owning an e-book" (Jabr 2013). Participants in a study she conducted on this phenomenon admitted that if they enjoyed an electronic book, they would go out and buy the paper version. Perhaps that's why, according to the *Los Angeles Times*, 95 percent of sales for *Diary of a Wimpy Kid #10: Old School* were in print (Kellogg 2015).

Independent Reading Tips

- Make sure your classroom library is stocked with all kinds of nonfiction texts, including magazines, video game manuals, and other fun stuff!
- Play Genre Bingo (see page 163)
- Have students interview friends and family to find out what genres they read every day.
- Reward students for trying a new genre or subgenre they've never read before.

It's heartening to see the viability of beloved print books validated. Study after study show the benefits of teaching from both the page *and* the screen, as long as that instruction thoughtfully incorporates the affordances of both media—affordance meaning the strengths and weaknesses of technologies with respect to the possibilities they offer to the people who might use them (Gaver 1991). Dr. Maryanne Wolf has authored several important studies and has written multiple books about the reading brain's encounters with print vs. digital text. She encourages educators to be aware of the pitfalls of an approach to literacy that privileges the digital over the printed form: "An early immersion in reading that is largely online tends to reward certain cognitive skills, such as multitasking, and habituate the learner to immediate information gathering and quick attention shifts, rather than to deep reflection and original thought" (Wolf and Barzillai 2009). This would suggest the critical importance of building a foundation of reading printed books while being mindful of the enormous potential benefits of the "interactivity and convenience" of multimodal e-books (Schugar, Smith, and Schugar 2013).

It's important, even critical, to acknowledge the power that teachers and caregivers hold over shaping the reading and writing habits of children, but it's also important to step back and observe where a child's intuition guides him or her, whether it be the subject matter of independent reading choices or the text's mode of delivery (which, in some cases, could be a text message). While continuing to enjoy and honor the print book, educators must also look at the evolution of reading and figure out ways to create confident explorers of students. Now is the time to empower students with the tools they need to tame the wild text.

How Can We Help?

Technology may be in the forefront of education, but that does not mean that the best practices of traditional reading are being abandoned. Whether students are reading from paper or a tablet, the strategies teachers employ to develop strong readers grow out of the same foundation. As students begin to read widely, their interactions with text should include both traditional and digital forms, both literature and informational text. Preparing students for real world reading means ensuring that they get to experience all kinds of texts at all times of the day.

Modeling

Modeling interactions with text is essential when building skills to help students read widely. A kindergarten teacher may model a picture walk with a print or digital text, asking students to draw a picture of what they've learned with a mobile app and record their voice to narrate their illustration. A fifth grade teacher may use an interactive whiteboard to model how to color-code a text when reading in order to gather facts about a topic. Fifth graders can then open up an e-book in a digital library and tap on the screen to add color-coding to different parts of the text. Alternatively, fifth graders working in print reading materials may use a tablet to snap a picture of the print page and annotate that image using digital tools. Modeling reading behaviors for students helps connect reading instruction to the real world. Taking a moment to make a connection to one's own reading life can be as simple as "You won't believe what I saw written on a sign this morning. As I was driving to school today, the supermarket displayed a funny riddle that made me laugh out loud!" Bringing students into their teacher's reading life can show them how classroom reading skills are transferred into the real world.

Digital Reading At Home

Families understand the power of the smartphone in their pocket or the tablet in their children's hands, but they appreciate the guidance on how to use these tools for learning.

Families can benefit from strategic recommendations from teachers on how to use digital text to support reading at home. We can leverage these interactions and provide resources for families with access to technology.

Honoring Cultures

Families have different levels of comfort with technology and a varying degree of understanding when it comes to the power of educational technology as a learning tool. In order to navigate the school and home relationship successfully, it is essential for teachers and their schools to honor the traditions and cultures of families. This includes developing an understanding of the way families interact with reading materials at home.

Resources for Reading at Home

- Newsela
- YouTube (search "read alouds")
- StorylineOnline®
- OceanHouse Media
- News-O-Matic
- iBooks® Children Category

Providing opportunities for students to take home print books should go hand in hand with sending lists of strong reading apps or online resources to families. In addition to finding a balance between print and digital text in the classroom, schools can support families as they begin to navigate the waters of traditional and digital text. Families should feel confident that their smartphones or tablets can be used to give their child easy access to high-quality text. Families should also feel comfortable continuing to read to their children the way they were read to and embracing home traditions of reading print.

Screen Time

A long-anticipated revision of the American Academy of Pediatrics (AAP) recommendations on screen time, first released in 1999, reflects a more nuanced view of technology's influence on early childhood development. Instead of discouraging any access to screens for children under age two, the 2016 guidelines now include this caveat: "Avoid solo media use in this age group" (3).

This recommendation acknowledges studies that show that very young children can benefit from educational videos or apps if a parent or caregiver interacts with the screen alongside the child, reinforcing vocabulary words or pointing out key details and events. Older children in the two-to-five age range should limit screen time to an hour per day and, once again, AAP recommends a shared experience between the child and parent or caregiver. It's possible for children at this age to transfer the knowledge they may gain from screens to the real world, but that possibility increases when another person capable of reinforcing what they are seeing and hearing is involved in the exchange.

The teachers of the world now face an even greater responsibility to facilitate the meaningful transfer of knowledge from screens to sponge-like learners as the number of devices multiply in our classrooms. A 2015 report issued by the Organisation for Economic Co-operation and Development reaffirmed what so many educators, parents, and students already know to be true: "Technology can amplify great teaching, but great technology cannot replace poor teaching." Dr. Kentaro Toyama of the University of Michigan School of Information adds his voice to the growing chorus of educators who caution against viewing an increase in screen time as a panacea for lackluster classroom performance and engagement: "Technology's primary effect is to amplify human forces, so in education, technologies amplify whatever pedagogical capacity is already there" (2015). All the more reason for us to embrace our adult learning in the intersection of technology and print-based reading experiences so that we can accompany our students on this great journey and not be left behind.

Research Spotlight

Researchers Lee and Barron (2015) found that parents who often used digital technology for personal learning had children who used educational media more often, highlighting an important association between parents' and children's media use. This suggests that designing intergenerational learning opportunities can be especially powerful.

Subscription-Based Digital Libraries:

- EPIC!
- News-O-Matic
- Reading Rainbow
- DK Readers
- Teacher Created Materials Explor-eBook

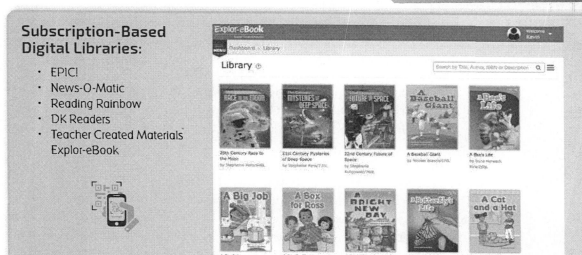

A Blended World

Students with access to both traditional print materials and digital tools intuitively combine these mediums. In elementary school, a student may look up the definition of a new word in an online dictionary to hear the correct pronunciation or to better understand its meaning. In middle school, students may respond to reading by creating a video blog that shares their opinions of a book. In high school, students may flip through a textbook and pause to look up a definition using their smartphone. As students dive into this blended world, educators need to be comfortable with the notion that print and digital text can support each other.

So, how do educators make the most of this blended world? First, teachers must be observant of their students, reaching them where they are and using their noticings to take students to the next level. This could include placing QR codes on the backs of new print books, allowing students to scan and view a book trailer created by their peers. This digital and print connection can be used before deciding whether to commit to reading this new book. Students can still experience the joy of sitting on a rug in the corner of their classroom and hearing their

Resources for Early Digital Readers

- **Website:** Joan Ganz Cooney Center
- **Book:** *Tap, Click, Read* by Lisa Guernsey and Michael H. Levine
- **Article:** "Screen Time" by Lisa Guernsey

teacher read a book aloud. In a blended world, students may respond to the read aloud by recording their thoughts in an interactive reading journal.

Students who read widely embrace both digital and print text and read across genres. They dive into books delightedly, with a sense of freedom and personal empowerment. Students of today and of the future know that flipping through pages of a book and tapping the screen of an interactive text are both ways in which active readers experience text. They also understand that they can tap a word on their tablet and hear it pronounced for them or get a vocabulary word explained quickly and clearly. Readers today are absorbing print in ways that make them more fully engaged with text. It is not an "either/or." They don't see reading online or off-line as separate or isolated interactions with text but part of their reading tool belt that can be used to tame the wild text in front of them. The same is true for their interaction with genre variety. A poem leads to a discovery of the poet's life, which leads to a blog post about the poet's love of music, which leads to a news article about the uses of poetry to sustain people during difficult times. Taming the wild text means that wide reading is accepted, understood, and embraced.

Dear Families,   _____

Children who read widely are able to access different types of text during each day—both inside and outside the classroom. As parents and caregivers, you can help model a love of and an appreciation for a wide range of reading materials. You may gravitate toward a favorite genre in the same way your children do, but the conversations you can have with your children about your own reading life will help them understand their journeys as readers.

In your home, take a moment to talk about your favorites—how you love to read historical fiction but will try out a science fiction book if it is highly recommended by a special family member. After reading an interesting news article on your smartphone, pause to have a conversation with your children about how you love reading text that teaches you something new or makes you wonder. When you read aloud with your children each evening, introduce an unexpected text like a magazine article on a heroic figure or an interactive storybook on a topic they have never heard of before. You can even read a funny cartoon or a silly note from Grandma. If you love sports and always check the scores, refer to this as reading, too. You have the power to introduce a range of text to your children to help them read widely.

Keep a record on your refrigerator of all the different types of text your family reads: cereal boxes, game instructions, and text messages all count. Use the "Genre Bingo" board as a fun way to keep track. Ask your children questions such as the following:

- What new kinds of reading would you like to do together?

- What is a type of reading you haven't tried yet?

- What is your favorite genre?

It is important that we value all the many kinds of reading our children do and want to do. Reading Widely, the first of our Five Habits, will soon become something they do every day.

With appreciation,

Queridas familias: _____

Los niños que leen extensamente logran comprender de mejor manera distintos tipos de textos: tanto dentro como fuera del aula. Como padres y cuidadores, ustedes pueden ayudar a demostrar un amor y un aprecio hacia una amplia gama de materiales de lectura. Tal vez ustedes, al igual que sus hijos, tengan un género preferido, pero las conversaciones que tengan con sus hijos acerca de sus propias experiencias como lectores ayudarán a que sus hijos entiendan los pasos que tomarán como lectores.

Tomen un momento en casa para conversar acerca de sus géneros preferidos: por ejemplo, cómo les encanta leer ficción histórica, pero leerían un libro de ciencia ficción si cierto pariente se los recomienda. Después de leer en su móvil inteligente un artículo interesante, tomen una pausa para conversar con sus hijos acerca de cómo les encanta leer textos educativos o textos que los dejen pensando. Cuando lean en voz alta cada noche con sus hijos, hagan uso de un texto inesperado, tal como un artículo de revista acerca de una figura heroica o un libro interactivo que se trate de un tema que sus hijos no conozcan. Incluso pueden leer una viñeta chistosa o una nota graciosa de su abuelita. Si les gustan los deportes y siempre comprueban los resultados, háganles saber que esto también es lectura. Ustedes tienen la capacidad de presentarle a sus hijos una variedad de textos para ayudarlos a leer extensamente.

Registren en la puerta del refrigerador todos los tipos de texto que su familia lee. Las cajas de cereal, las instrucciones de juegos y los mensajes de texto son todos ejemplos válidos. Mantengan un registro de manera divertida usando el tablero de "Genre Bingo". Háganles preguntas a sus hijos tales como:

- ¿Qué nuevos tipos de lectura te gustaría que viéramos juntos?
- ¿Cuál es un tipo de lectura que no has realizado?
- ¿Cuál es tu género preferido?

Es importante que valoremos las clases de lectura que nuestros hijos realizan y las que quieren realizar. Leer extensamente [Read Widely], el primero de nuestros Cinco hábitos [Five Habits], pronto será algo que harán diariamente.

Con agradecimiento,

Reading Critically

Samantha, a kindergartner, already knows what she likes. She knows that one book makes her laugh with her sister, and another is the one she likes to read before bedtime. This kindergartener is a critical reader, perhaps the most critical reader of all, perusing picture books with the same intensity that, years later, a high school student uses to peruse a longer text.

Jose is in seventh grade and is a reader of the news. He reads with a critical eye, looking at the author's perspective to see what his or her point of view is. In the age of quick digital publishing, where anyone anywhere has the opportunity to post or print their thinking, students must develop critical reading skills.

Samantha, at the age of five, is brimming with opinions. Jose, at age 12, is on the alert for what is falsified news and what is validated. The critical reader is building ideas and perspectives as he or she reads, using evidence from the text and the world to prove or disprove an idea. This is reading critically.

Both the kindergartener and middle school student can examine text as critical thinkers. As readers of varied genres and text types, students need to be prepared to critically examine the text that pops up on their screen or appears when they turn the page. This chapter examines how students can interact with digital and print text to read with a critical eye at every age. This is a crucial skill for students asked to tame the wild text across all platforms.

Teachers can help English language learners be assertive and bold in their own critical reading even as they decode simpler text in English. Teachers can provide students with books in their native language, so they can become experts about subjects they love. Even when reading simpler text, ELLs should not be silenced. They should express their perspective on these texts as they read. Simpler texts can also invite complex discussion, providing authentic opportunities for oral language practice.

For below level learners, reading critically is something they are often separated from as they are asked to memorize vocabulary and stick close to highly structured language controlled text. But it is really important for them to feel a part of the reading community and to express their opinions. If they are struggling with verbal skills, they can express likes and dislikes online with thumbs up or thumbs down emojis. If they would like to share an opinion of a character, they can draw the character using color in ways that convey meaning, highlighting with bright colors the important parts of the character's profile (e.g., a bright red heart). Reading critically is an adventure for all of our students.

Setting the Stage for Critical Thinking

Just as writing benefits from the good counsel of teachers and fellow writers, a child's reading life is enriched by seeking out others' interpretations of a book. This search's reward is a sense of community surrounding the book, almost like a force field of ideas that could not exist without the involvement of other enthusiastic readers. Constructing new ideas about what is read depends on the level of trust students have in their learning environment. New thoughts may not be fully formed, but they will grow as students read more and spend time speaking and listening. Inquiry-based instruction creates an environment ripe for opinion seeking in the form of turn-and-talk discussions with a partner or open-ended questions that encourage engagement and curiosity. And nothing makes an opinion-rich environment thrive more than a true "windows and mirrors" text collection at a reader's fingertips. As previously discussed, when children see themselves in a text, their engagement level skyrockets, and they are more apt to share their thoughts with others who may not necessarily see a mirror but are happy to look into a wondrous window and find not only a good story but also a friend.

Teachers can also help students seek out opinions based on substance rather than whims, a critical skill they will need when navigating the wilds of social media where opinions are ubiquitous but sound evidence for holding such opinions is scant (at best). Students will begin to understand that they can seek and share strongly held opinions about a text without succumbing to rigid declarations of "best" and "worst" or even that classic debate deflator: "Because I said so!" Students will begin to view their peers and teachers as reading role models with whom they can share substantive, evidence-based opinions, thoughtfully constructed to broaden understanding of multiple perspectives. With any luck, the sheer variety of interpretations will help them understand that the best kind of writing holds multitudes of meanings for every reader who dares to take the plunge.

Having students share their favorite books and post excerpts is great, but teachers can take this a step further by encouraging students to post about why they don't like a character, what excerpt drove them crazy, and the point in the text when they really started to question the author. Students can create book trailers and book reviews in visual forms to post online, encouraging vibrant discussion among their peers. Students can even do "face offs," debating elements in texts by creating one minute videos to show their point of view.

Examining Texts and Websites

When students dive into print text, they should be able to speak to the authority of the author on a particular subject. A kindergarten student may be able to talk about how the author of their book on trucks has also written books on cars and boats, so he must be an expert on different types of transportation. A sixth grader may be able to point to the copyright date in a book on cell phones and realize it was published too long ago to provide a reader with current information.

These types of judgments will not come naturally to all readers. Teachers should strategically introduce this level of evaluation during targeted whole class mini lessons and small group intervention. Modeling with think alouds gives students a window into a teacher's thought process and can be used to help students understand the behaviors of strong, active readers. Whether an excerpt of text is placed under a document camera or a website is displayed on an interactive whiteboard, students should observe the teacher as he or she thinks aloud. The teacher should model his or her thought process with questions and comments, such as *What else has this author published? This information will help me understand if he is an expert on this topic. When was this article written? Knowing the publication date will help me determine if this article is still relevant and up-to-date.*

When students type a keyword or term into a search bar, the results that appear on their screen will require them to think critically. Teachers can model this process by thinking aloud after conducting a search. They can walk students through their thought processes for picking and choosing between a list of websites in a set of search results. Students can see how teachers make a snap judgment to rule out certain search results and how they dig deeper into other search results to evaluate their authority. In this digital age, students have to sort through information that may be very helpful or not relevant at all.

Examining a text for authority and clarity is just as important in the digital realm as it is in print. As students examine a website to evaluate the information presented, they should take several things into consideration. To begin, teachers will want to show students how to look for the organization behind the website. Just as students think about the author of a book, children should be able to identify (independently or with teacher guidance) what organization is providing information on a particular website. Discussions about the subtle differences between similar information found on two different websites can help illustrate

Independent Reading Tips

- Make a box or online folder of "Our Favorites," and encourage your students to curate throughout the year.

- Acknowledge when your students do not agree with an author, and have a focused conversation on the disagreement.

- Do a point/counterpoint talk-show format of the read aloud to agree or disagree with points in the text.

- Hold mock debates, taking the point of view of a character or an opposing point of view.

the range of authorship behind different websites. As students examine specific content on a website, they should look for the name of additional authors and discuss the information they've found.

As with all of the strategies presented in this book, modeling is key. Students must watch teachers tame the wild text in order to do it themselves. Students do not have to be proficient, independent readers to benefit from a conversation on evaluating print and digital sources. Early elementary school students can have a conversation about why the San Diego Zoo's website has more trustworthy information than a person's blog post about their visit to the zoo. Upper elementary school students can look at search results with teachers and determine which sources are trustworthy.

Think-Aloud Questions

Questions you might ask yourself as you model and think aloud to students:

- *Who is in charge of this website?*
- *What is the quality of the information?*
- *Do they have a bias or a strong opinion on this topic?*
- *I wonder why the author chose this word.*
- *I wonder what type of experience the reporter has with this topic.*
- *I wonder why the author wrote about this topic.*
- *I wonder why the reporter chose to interview this person for their article.*

Evaluating Sources

Students today are challenged to evaluate content presented on multiple platforms. From picture books to blog posts, digital tools give students access to an enormous amount of content on a daily basis. It is essential for students to develop skills that will help them navigate this sea of text. *Higher order thinking* is more than a buzzword; it refers to an elevated interaction with content where students develop the ability to evaluate sources with a critical eye.

Vocabulary to Use with Critical Readers

Depending on the grade level of students that you work with and the focus of your lessons, here are vocabulary words you can introduce when helping students read critically.

- *evaluate*
- *verify*
- *authority*
- *bias*
- *facts*
- *opinion*

When readers think critically about the choices an author has made—from word choice to text organization—they are reading at a higher level. Critical readers of print and digital text are able to sort through text on a page and on a screen. They are able to use text evidence to support their thinking and determine the meaning behind a passage.

Author Bias

In the past, readers of all ages may have taken it for granted that a piece of print text was vetted under the eye of a skillful editor. Today's students need to be prepared for a world where anyone with an Internet connection can hit *submit* and see their work published online. This is an exciting time for writers who now have easier ways to tell their stories, share information, and connect with an audience. This is also an important time for us to dedicate a portion of our instruction to thinking critically about the *who* behind a piece of writing.

Reading critically means students understand an author's purpose and bias. First graders should be able to articulate why an author wrote a book on polar bears or why an author chose the word *mischievous* to describe the main character in a read aloud. Fourth graders should be able to think about a reporter's background when they read a feature article and question the choices that the author made. All of this happens with the guidance of a teacher, who strategically thinks aloud to model these critical reading skills.

Developing the skill to evaluate and question a source can happen in whole class discussions in kindergarten as students wonder aloud about an author. Our youngest students can ponder questions, such as *Why would this author write a book about the forest?* or *What do we know about where they grew up?* It can also happen in upper elementary school classrooms where students may explore a handful of texts on the same topic during an investigation on author's bias. These students may discuss questions, such as *Why would the writer of this article choose to interview the captain of the ship and not someone who worked below deck?* Educators guide students into these discussions and explorations to help them learn how to tame the wild text with a critical eye.

Today, it is much easier to locate articles in local newspapers thanks to the websites of these local news organizations. Anyone with an Internet connection can view content published in small towns and large cities around the world. After a notable sports game, like a playoff for a national title, visit a local newspaper's website to access their version of the game's highlights. Students can examine two perspectives of a story by working with multiple news sources. Teachers don't have to wait until the morning after Game Seven of the World Series to try this activity. Any Sunday morning coverage of a college football matchup can give them plenty to work with.

Primary Sources

A great shift from digital to print text is to examine texts from long ago. A primary source document is a piece of writing, image, photograph, or artifact created by a person during a particular time in the past. Blog posts, which offer an opinion or response to events in the past, can even be considered primary source documents.

21st Century Reading Tip

Many famous speeches and other primary source documents can be found in video or audio form online. Even if the speech was written before this technology came into play, you can hear other people reading the speech aloud. Just try searching for Gettysburg Address on YouTube to see examples.

Although there is nothing quite the same as holding a document in one's hand or feeling an object from long ago, digital tools make it easier than ever to access primary source documents, images, or artifacts. Museums, libraries, and archives are digitizing their resources and developing online search portals, so users anywhere in the world can access their content. There are a variety of archives online, and even a simple Internet search can help teachers find images to share with students. As students develop the capacity to evaluate sources, incorporating primary sources into this skill development is a fantastic way to establish cross-curricular connections. Students can evaluate a photograph from the American Civil Rights Movement by discussing the angle of the camera or the photographer's decision to capture one action instead of another. Even the youngest students can examine the colors in an image and discuss the mood or how the image makes them feel. Older elementary students may examine a piece of text like a letter from Lewis and Clark to President Thomas Jefferson. Students of all ages can look at a picture presented on their tablet, projected onto a screen, or within a textbook on their desk. The authors of primary source documents have their own motivations and biases. They make strategic choices to include some information and omit other details—just like the authors of a novel or memoir.

Locating Primary-Source Documents

- Library of Congress
- National Archives
- LIFE Photo Archive

Activity: Primary Source Analysis

Goals:
- Students will examine a primary source document or image.

Preparation:
- Choose a primary source document that connects with a unit of study and is appropriate for the students in front of you. This could include an image of the Great Plains during the Dust Bowl or a building of historical significance in your town snapped 20, 50, or 100 years ago.

Steps for Success:

1. Display the primary source document using an interactive whiteboard or a document camera. You may also have each student open up the primary source document on a personal screen, like a tablet or a laptop.

2. Provide a bit of background information for the image, or review main ideas from previous social studies lessons. You may say to students, "We have been studying and reading about this topic. Today, we are going to read an image by looking closely at it."

3. Depending on the group of students you are working with, you may decide to linger on the term *primary source document* or simply explain that the image you are looking at is from long ago.

4. Model how you examine the image, and share what you see. You may start with "I notice" or "I wonder." After you have modeled your initial thinking, pose a question to the class and ask them to share their response with a partner.

5. Provide a second image or group of images for students to examine with a partner. You may want to provide specific guiding questions or an open-ended set of questions for them to think about.

6. Once your students have had the chance to examine the primary source document with their partner, bring the class together for a whole group discussion.

Gathering Information

Students who interact with print and digital text should be able to read critically to gather information. Children reading as researchers can collect facts, support opinions, and learn about the world around them. The strategies used by readers to gather information from both print and digital text will vary over the course of a school year. Their purpose for reading can include gathering information to write as researchers. Teachers can model skills for reading critically by diving into mentor texts with students and demonstrating how to gather information to include in their own model writing.

Readers who start with questions are empowered. Their reading is more active. They are looking at the text not as a morass of print but as a treasure hunt, a way to focus their thinking and go on a search for their wondering. First grade students may read a print or a digital text to find a fun fact about a new topic. Older readers may be on the hunt for an answer to a question they have as they research a topic.

Critical readers make plans for these questions. They may take notes on their top three wonderings and then do searches through the text for them. They may use a sticky note or a tech tool to post question marks as they read and then go back to those question marks and freewrite off them to jump start them into a great piece of writing.

Students researching from a print text can use elements of text structure and organization to aid in their search for information. The table of contents, bold vocabulary words, and graphics spread throughout a book will all help students read to learn about a new topic.

 Research Spotlight

Researchers have looked at the way readers interact with digital text. Simpson, Walsh, and Rowsell (2013) found that reading on an iPad strengthened multi-directional text experiences for readers. This is because readers could move from one place to another in a digital text to make meaning of what they have read. The research found that reading pathways were influenced by touch-screen capabilities.

EdTech Spotlight:

The ACES Framework is the tool Monica uses to discuss deeper learning with scannable technology. It stands for **Access, Curate, Engage** and **Share.**

You can curate resources by locating the best websites, videos, and audio clips for your students. Once you've chosen your favorite online spots for students to visit, connect those links to a QR code, and share it with students. Students can scan the code using a QR reader app that can be downloaded onto any device with Internet access.

How can you curate resources with QR Codes?

- Examine your learning goals for students. Perhaps you want your students to learn about the differences between biomes or explore what life was like in your town 100 years ago.
- Find the resources you want students to read, watch, or listen to, like a video on the tundra or a website on the Dust Bowl.
- Open up a QR code creator (like QRstuff.com) and copy the link to the video or website into the appropriate location on the QR code generator website. It's free to use, and you can download your newly personalized QR code onto your computer to print or display for students.

Our favorite QR reader app is the i-nigma Reader since it is available for multiple devices.

The skills students develop while navigating print text can transfer to their exploration of digital text, where many similar features are included and enhanced for readers. Making this transfer of skills from print to digital text should happen through a combination of natural exploration of text and explicit instruction. This will guide students to a deeper understanding of text features.

Interacting with digital information provides students with an increasingly popular way to gather information. With digital texts, students can tap on a word to hear it pronounced or view a definition. In many reading apps for tablets and smartphones, students can use an annotation tool to highlight a sentence or a passage. There is often the option to tap and add a note for future reference. On a mobile app, where students interact with the page using a touch screen, these digital interactions become intuitive and expected for readers. In the same way students would put a sticky note on a page, they are now tapping their screens to summarize new information with a digital note.

Technology tools place a wide range of multimedia into the hands of both teachers and students. Multimedia can include video, images, text, and interactive diagrams. Podcasts are a form of multimedia that can place audio recordings at students' fingertips to connect children to a world of information. Listening to an episode of a science podcast can inspire students to read about a new topic. A podcast episode can also connect students to an instant read aloud full of sound effects and captivating narration. Children of all ages can access stories and information through video content. High-interest media can grab the attention of students, provide background knowledge, extend thinking, and reinforce content. Strengthen listening skills with students of all ages by effectively introducing multimedia use.

The LitLoop

Pam often highlights the LitLoop in her discussions of multimedia with teachers. The LitLoop demonstrates the ways reading, writing, speaking, listening, and viewing all come together, so students can approach literacy learning with a variety of skills.

Activity: Keyword Search

Goal:

- Students will search online using keywords to gather information on a topic.

Preparation:

- Decide on a topic and search terms you will use. Be sure that both will produce results you can work with during a whole class discussion. For example, if your students are completing an inquiry project on endangered species, your search terms may be *polar bear, polar bear habitat, polar bear diet,* or *polar bear threats* instead of *Why is a polar bear endangered?, Where does a polar bear live?,* or *things a polar bear eats.*

- Type these search terms into your search engine (ex. Google™, Bing®) so you can anticipate some of the results that will pop up on the screen.

Steps for Success:

1. Model your search for students. Talk to students about how keywords are more effective than complete sentences. You may want to create a T-chart of exemplars and non-exemplars similar to the Keyword Search sheet on page 165.

2. Send students off to brainstorm questions and keywords for their search. They may work independently or with a partner depending on the type of activity you have designed.

3. After students have brainstormed their keywords, show them how you will gather information as you read. It is important to model how you skim or read a page on the Internet to gather information and record what you've found. Depending on the age and experience of your students, you may incorporate a conversation about evaluating sources or appropriate citations into this discussion.

4. As students work, you may decide to pause the class and provide an extra search tip. ("Don't forget to read the captions of images and diagrams to seek out more information on your topic.")

5. After students have spent time gathering information, bring them back together to share their reflections and discuss any obstacles they faced while searching for information.

Note Taking with Digital Tools

Taking notes with digital tools completely alters the traditional experience of reading to gather information. Note taking with digital tools is a practice teachers can introduce to students when they are reading traditional or digital print. Digital note taking tools let students capture their thoughts while writing in a new way. Students can record their voice, snap a picture, and organize their thoughts in digital notebooks and folders. Teachers used to ask students to color-code index cards, but now students can use digital tools to change the color of text or add color to a digital note to help organize thinking. Instead of searching for highlighters, students can take notes in different colors, add written comments or voice recordings to the page, and insert relevant links or images. With digital tools, students can move their notes from one side of the screen or one part of a document to another. This transforms the way that students interact with their devices and the way they interact with text.

When students create a digital space to take notes, they should use a platform that is accessible from any web browser. They can use a tablet, a computer, or a smartphone to log in on a web browser and see all of their notes right where they left off. In early elementary school, students may collect facts using a digital sticky note app to keep their notes all in one place. Upper elementary school students may use a mind-mapping tool or a graphic organizer to collect their thoughts before writing a research paper.

In the same way teachers notice and honor the learning styles of students, digital tools can be used in the classroom to determine what works best for different students. As students read to gather information on a topic, notice how they interact with digital note taking tools. Providing options for students to gather

Digital Tools for Note Taking

- Google Docs
- Evernote
- Notability
- Simplenote

and organize their notes lets them pick and choose how to interact with text and capture their thinking. Giving students choice hardly means there is a free-for-all in your classroom.

Voice-to-Text Apps

- Dragon Dictation
- Speechnotes
- Evernote

Audio recording and voice-to-text technology have transformed the way students take notes with digital devices. They can now turn the pages of the book sitting in their lap while recording an interesting fact or question they have using the digital device in their hand. With a voice-recorder app, students can record audio clips, save them, and then search through them by date and time. Students may prefer to use a voice-to-text tool that captures their audio and turns it into sentences. Audio recording and voice-to-text are great options to use with students of any age or ability. This process is less disruptive to the flow of reading than stopping to compose a few sentences. It can also support English language learners who may be comfortable talking about their learning but struggle to write a response or jot down a note as they read.

Writing from Multiple Sources

Writing and reading go hand in hand. Writers can use the skills they develop as readers to strengthen their compositions. An understanding of how to navigate text, gather information, and cite sources is essential for critical readers. By exposing students to abundant variety in text, they become more capable of writing powerfully. Students who are asked to read critically often have a clear purpose for writing about reading. Students who read critically are looking for something. They are searching for information to support their thinking. This happens whether they are writing an informational text profiling a historical figure or composing a literary essay comparing the theme in two texts.

Writing from sources will look different in classrooms of early and upper elementary school students. Students writing from sources know that a picture in a read-aloud book and a line in an online encyclopedia both provide useful information to support their thinking. Teachers can encourage higher order thinking by asking questions, such as:

- What information can you learn from this image?
- What part of the text does this image connect to?
- Why do you think the author included this image?
- Can you explain this information to a friend?
- Where can you go to find more information on this topic?

Children of all ages should think about the way they are gathering information from content they've read, listened to, or viewed. Providing opportunities to write from sources gives students the chance to demonstrate their understanding while making connections to text.

In order for students to write from sources, they need to have access to quality texts. Searching for quality texts online and off-line can be a daunting task for teachers. You want to find texts that are complex and rich, at a level your students can investigate independently and with support, and that capture the interests of your students. This means that the texts you locate and share with students will likely be differentiated based on complexity, structure, and topic.

Tasks Before Apps

Monica likes to use the phrase *tasks before apps* to describe the idea of putting the learning first when designing these types of activities for students. If you want students to collect multimedia and keep track of their sources, you'll want to pick a tool that gives them the ability to easily organize this information.

In addition to high quality text, students writing from sources should have access to both digital and print text. As they grow as critical readers, students will need to become just as comfortable gathering information from a blog post accessed on a smartphone as they are searching the index of a print book in the library.

Today's learner is writing from sources or using evidence to inform or make an argument. While there is still room to help students develop a deep sense of voice and purpose in narrative writing, informational and explanatory writing is more in line with what they will be asked to produce in the real world. To be college and career ready, students need the ability to gather and synthesize information and introduce others to their line of thinking. They must be able to do so in writing while making use of source materials.

Another key skill when writing from sources is the ability to reflect on the facts that they have gathered, summarized, and reported on. Students must develop their own interpretation of the raw research materials they have amassed. Teachers can guide students to ask and answer questions, such as:

- What does it mean?
- Where do we go from here in our search?

- How can we best use the data and information to make a new determination about our subject?

Citizens are more powerful when they can gather information from many different sources, formulate their own informed opinions, and present those opinions to the world in ways that influence others. This necessitates a reexamination of the type of writing educators are asking students to produce. Are teachers too heavily focused on narrative writing? Are they scaffolding for students as they synthesize facts to create their own understandings? Are teachers giving students enough time and opportunity to write their understandings for real audiences? The answers to these questions will help determine whether young writers have the skills they need to succeed in the world beyond school.

Digital Tools to Organize Thinking

The following tools can be used to help students organize their thinking:

- **Popplet**: This concept mapping tool lets users add a range of media.
- **BrainPOP® Make-a-Map**: Students can use this tool as they gather and organize information from BrainPOP videos.
- **Padlet**: Students can use this tool independently or collaboratively to collect their thinking about a topic.

Padlet

Below are tips for how to help students organize writing from sources.

- Provide students with text sets. These collections of books and articles that match up fiction and nonfiction will help even the youngest students see how reading multiple texts will enliven their understanding. Along with these texts, ask a guiding question to teach them how to read across the genres. For example, "What is a big wondering you have, and how can you explore it across these four texts?"

- Create an online or off-line portfolio where students can photograph the covers of books they have searched to keep track of their sources.

- Use note taking-apps with your older students, and give them one article and one poem on the same subject. Ask, "How is this subject treated the same or differently by two different genre writers?" Have them take notes and then share with a partner.

- For younger students, give them poster board and a set of three books on the same subject. Ask them, "What three things do you learn by reading all three books?" Students can then create a visual on their learning and share it with a partner.

- After a period of intensive independent reading from sources, let your students freewrite before composing a thesis statement. After the freewrite, students can highlight a line or two that reflects their point of view. Then, have them use that line and go back to their sources to "prove" its worth.

Tools with Easy and Automatic Citations

- Spark Page
- Shadow Puppet Edu
- Haiku Deck

Incorporating Text Citations

As students begin to respond to text through written responses, teachers have the opportunity to cultivate digital citizenship skills. Digital citizenship instruction is becoming increasingly popular in schools across the country. These schools understand just how essential it is to prepare students for a world where they have to interact with online content and communicate through digital tools.

The task of teaching students how to be good digital citizens—navigating the web in a safe and appropriate manner—is often taught in isolation by a technology teacher, a librarian, or a media specialist. In the reading classroom, teachers have the opportunity to introduce students to digital citizenship skills in an authentic manner. Whether taking advantage of teachable moments or strategically incorporating lessons on this topic, educators can include conversations about citations when students are writing from sources.

Learning how to cite from sources will look different across the grade levels. Younger students may watch their teacher make a note about the page number where a fun fact about an endangered species was found. Older students may use a modified MLA or APA guide as they develop a reference section for a multipage e-book on a period of American history. Introducing the idea of *giving credit where credit is due* can become part of regular conversations with students. Building this understanding at a young age can help students transfer this knowledge to more sophisticated citation of sources in the future.

Dear Families,   _____

As your children dive into reading, it is important for them to know they are the bosses of their reading! Especially in this era of "fake news," we want to be sure our kids feel confident noting what feels real and what does not. Children have opinions about text. They wonder about who is in charge of a website or what the author of their favorite book has in mind. Critical readers are always alert and always reading with questions. We hope you will model this with your children at home, whether you are reading a comic or a news article.

Wonder aloud when you see an infographic printed in a newspaper or when you flip to the About the Author section of a beloved picture book. Children will watch you think critically about what you have read. Express your opinion! Let your child know whether you like something you've read. Bringing your children into your thought process can help them develop the confidence needed to question and analyze the world around them. The following questions can help:

- What do you think of this book we are reading?

- Why do you think the author wrote it?

- What is your opinion of the author's ideas?

Good luck, and thank you for helping to build the Five Habits for your children!

With appreciation,

Queridas familias: _____

A medida que sus hijos se zambullen en la lectura, ¡es importante que sepan que son los jefes de su propia lectura! Queremos asegurarnos de que nuestros hijos se sientan con la confianza de poder distinguir cuáles textos parecen auténticos y cuáles no, sobre todo en esta era de noticias ficticias. Los niños tienen opiniones acerca de los textos. Se preguntan quién se encarga de un sitio web o qué tiene en mente el autor de sus libros favoritos. Los lectores críticos siempre están alertas y siempre se hacen preguntas cuando leen. Ya sea que lean una viñeta o un artículo de noticias, esperamos que ustedes les demuestren esta práctica a sus hijos.

Pregúntense en voz alta cuando vean una infografía en un periódico o cuando echen un vistazo a la sección Acerca de un autor de un libro muy apreciado. Los niños observarán que piensan críticamente acerca de lo que acaban de leer. ¡Expresen su opinión! Háganle saber si algo que han leído les gusta o no. Darle a sus hijos la oportunidad de que participen en su razonamiento les ayudará a desarrollar la confianza precisa para cuestionar y analizar el mundo que los rodea. Las siguientes preguntas podrían ayudar:

- ¿Qué piensas de este libro que estamos leyendo?

- ¿Para qué lo escribió el autor?

- ¿Qué opinas de las ideas del autor?

¡Buena suerte y muchas gracias por ayudarnos a que sus hijos desarrollen los Cinco hábitos [Five Habits]!

Con agradecimiento,

Reading Deeply

David, a fifth grader, is poring over Bud, Not Buddy. This is the second time he has read this book. Anora asks her literature circle if they are as surprised as she is at the way The Tiger Rising is unfolding. She returns to a page where she sees a character changing and shares a quote with the group. Gideon pulls up a picture on his tablet to show his reading partner the setting of his historical fiction novel, fascinated by the details.

These students are reading deeply. They are reading with passion. They are invested in the characters and immersed in the story. Our students can tame the wild text when they think of it as a companion, as something they may want to return to. They see themselves in the story, growing and learning alongside the characters. This is reading deeply.

This chapter will discuss ways to help students read deeply. Students who think deeply about their reading can ask questions, share favorite books, and talk about what they have learned. They dive deeper into the text, turning ideas around and rolling them in their minds to unpack further discoveries. Reading deeply is reading with emotion and responding with feeling but still using text evidence to bolster a personal connection.

Students who read deeply connect their thoughts, experiences, and questions to what is happening in a text and feel passionately about what they are reading. They think about what they've read even after they've finished reading.

Teachers must provide English language learners with a chance to fall in love with texts in their native languages and in English. Consider providing ELLs with a copy of a class favorite in their native language, and invite them to join a book club in order to dive deeper into the text with peers. Let the power of reading deeply energize and inspire all students.

For below level learners, perhaps the text they connect with most deeply is the text with pictures only or a quirky comic book. They can feel the power of reading deeply with these "easier" texts. Teachers should not force upon them a "harder" book because they feel that the student must progress at that moment. Allow students to experience what it means to savor the text in their own way, at their own pace.

Reading Deeply Is Diving Down

Beyond the expectations for student reading responses, children should feel that there is personal depth in their reading experience. They may be pursuing a deeper question or finding out new ideas about a character. They may be discovering connections between overarching themes or just wanting to burrow deep in the comfort of the text. Reading deeply is often about falling in love with the text, examining it, and turning it over in one's mind. Below are of the ways that teachers can help students along a self-reflective path to deep reading.

- **Invite students to reread.** Place emphasis on the value of rereading simply because of a love of the text. The independent reading students do should be a catalyst for reading deeply. If a student loves a silly series like Captain Underpants, he or she can read deeply by connecting themes common to the first and most recent book in the series. If a student loves books about lions, he or she should have time to browse a stack of them and then share a favorite with a classmate. The child who reads the Harry Potter series more than once becomes invested in the lives of the characters. The first time, the student may be reading this book to discover the plot. But the second time, the deeper read may bring revelations about character motivation and small plot twists. Rereading must be encouraged!

- **Create fluid reading partnerships.** Students and teachers alike are encouraged to read deeply by others. Friends, family, peers, and colleagues push one's thinking when they come from a different perspective or they love a text in a different way. This enthusiasm can work wonders in a community of readers. Teachers should change the pairings in their classroom regularly so students get to read with different peers. Reading partnerships should be based on more than levels. For example, students can sign up for "Deep Reading Wednesdays," where they partner up with a friend who is reading a different book. Or partnerships can be created based on theme. Students reading books about friendship or loneliness can join together to discuss similarities and differences in their books. These conversations encourage students to share their enthusiasm and go deeper in their own texts.

- **Build passion for texts.** Mark the moments in which students are truly falling in love with something they are reading. Create bulletin boards titled "Our Passionate Reading Lives." Use language that redefines reading so that students are not just restating the *who, what, where, when,* and *why* of a text but are looking at the reasons why they love it. Use the read aloud to model how to stop and think for a moment about a line that contains personal significance. The Read-Aloud Planning Page on page 168 will help you prepare questions to ask yourself during the read aloud. Students can use your model as a guide, as they record the lines that they connect with the most and share them aloud at the end of a day.

- **Use writing burst exercises to enhance deep reading.** Have students use writing online and off-line as a way to further their relationships with the texts they are reading. Provide open-ended writing prompts, such as *write for five minutes about how this text is making you think differently* or *write for two minutes about what you would do if you were the character in this chapter.* Using small bursts of writing will help your students empathize with characters or find a piece of themselves in the story.

For our English language learners, reading deeply is a transformational opportunity to show off developing English skills while improving comprehension. Giving students permission to reread and dive deep encourages them to go beyond the decoding work and focus on the sensation that reading gives them. Make sure your English language learners have opportunities to do this with books in their native language. Reading in their native language helps ELLs become more and move confident as readers. English language learners can apply their expertise to other English texts that may pose more of a technical challenge. Allowing ELLs to reread books gives them the opportunity to think more about their comprehension instead of spending all of their time decoding. Teachers can provide easy access to read alouds in a basket or an online folder, so English language learners can revisit those texts on their own or with a partner. Students should be celebrated when their thinking goes beyond the surface, when they fall in love with a character or identify personally to a theme. Teachers can describe this to them as "strong reading," so they can feel and be part of what happens as they read, in either their primary or secondary language, when the words fall away and the book becomes a whole new world.

Building Stamina

Before students can examine text deeply, they must build the muscles they need as readers. Sustained reading activities can take place as a whole class and among independent readers. Children should have opportunities to sit and listen to an engaging read aloud or curl up with an independent reading book. These reading behaviors are not established overnight. Students need to strengthen their reading muscles through stamina-building activities.

Stamina building can occur from the first to the last day of school. Teachers may start the first week of second grade with a short read aloud on the rug. This routine will build up to sharing a complete chapter within a month or two. Teachers can communicate goals for stamina building by saying "Today, we are going to gather together for a read aloud of a favorite book. We are going to work on reading as a class for 10 minutes before heading back to our seats."

Students must also build stamina as independent readers. Kindergarten students may sit with a new book, flipping pages and thinking aloud about what is happening to the characters in the pictures. They may read with a partner for a few minutes and build their capacity to engage in independent reading activities over the course of the school year. For students in upper elementary classrooms, independent reading practice will look very different. Students should be able to sit with a chapter book or a news article on an open web browser for sustained periods of time. You may record the time on the board, so students know their goal for the day and can log their own reading minutes in their notebooks.

Independent Reading Tips

- Keep "Favorite Reread" books curated by your students in a book basket or online.

- Post a line, a paragraph, or an image from a favorite text on the wall, and have sticky notes handy for responses as students revisit the image or text more than once.

- Keep materials that encourage online or off-line highlighting within easy reach. This could include sticky notes, think marks, highlighters, colored pens, or digital devices.

- Have students write a response to the text in order to allow them to process their thinking and share their thoughts with a bigger audience.

Monitoring Independent Reading with Digital Tools

After students have developed stamina, a sense of ownership of their independent reading time is sure to follow. Students should cherish their time with books. They should set their own reading goals and read with passion. With technology, students have access to additional tools that can help them grow as independent readers. This may include timers on a tablet or digital reading journals. Successful independent readers need access to high-quality texts. This could include easy access to a digital library of chapter books or a current events website for kids. Students can commit to a daily book choice by posting their new book in a discussion thread or by sending their teacher a message through a learning management system like Google Classroom™ or Seesaw. Technology makes it easy for students to communicate with teachers and for teachers to monitor students' independence.

When students are reading independently, teachers can monitor their progress with online tools. A digital exit slip gives students a way to update teachers on their reading accomplishments for the day. Students can open up a tool like Socrative and respond to a prompt or a question that addresses the day's lesson. Students can type in their responses and send them straight to the teacher's device for review.

Teachers may also have students follow a protocol after completing an independent reading book. Students can fill out an online survey, answering a series of questions that has been prepared for them. Their responses will pop up on the teacher's screen, and he or she can monitor the student's comprehension. This helps in evaluating the appropriateness of students' book choices. If a student struggles with comprehension, he or she may need help choosing a high interest book that reads at a lower level. Similarly, if a student has no problem with comprehension questions and is soaring through reading, he or she needs to be directed toward more challenging books.

Inquiry-Based Book Clubs

Book clubs support the idea that students are reading to discover. Creating book clubs, or literature circles, around topics that make students wonder is a strong way to promote collaborative text talk and satisfy their curiosity. This common interest will inspire discovery and allow children of different reading levels to inquire and learn together.

Students of all ages should be able to identify the areas and topics they find interesting and would like to know more about. Teachers can make wondering a part of everyday teaching, from morning meetings to think alouds during the school day. Modeling how to pause and ask questions shows students that curiosity is a lifelong habit. Students can record questions on sticky notes or a collaborative document hosted online. Use the following concepts as guidelines for inquiry-based book clubs:

- Provide children with a say in how the clubs are organized. On a wall visible to all students, post students' wonderings across a period of time, and then have them use the wonderings to create a short term book club.

- Encourage clubs to use multimedia tools to express their thinking about the text.

Inquiry-based instruction gives students a clear sense of buy in. They are searching for answers to questions that they have identified as important to them. Their role in this process is to solve a problem or learn about a topic in which they are interested.

Curiosity drives so much of a child's reading and writing life, in and out of school, online and off-line. Unfortunately, the curiosity that is so evident in a child's early life is often suppressed in a school that values quiet obedience over active learning. In a study by Susan Engel, curiosity was measured by the number of questions asked in a two-hour period (Engel 2015). While kindergartners asked two to five questions in this time frame, many fifth graders went a full day without showing any signs of inquisitiveness. This disparity is a direct consequence of children's disengagement from reading, writing, and a love of learning. Teachers must do everything they can to help them keep hold of the most powerful tool for achievement: their own insatiable appetites for knowledge.

Digital Reading Responses

Readers who move beyond the surface level of the text can respond deeply to what they have read. Incorporating student choice into digital reading responses provides students with a sense of ownership of their work. In a tech-friendly classroom, teachers can provide students with multiple options for responding to reading. They may introduce one or two options at the beginning of the year and layer on additional choices as the school year progresses.

Although student readers may dive into blog posts to learn about a new topic, this is also a tool for writers. Think of blogging as similar to journaling. Children post their responses to a text in a chronological feed on a group blog. Student readers with access to a personal blog may post a few sentences here after reading independently each day. Literature circles may take turns posting updates on the class blog. Kidblog and WordPress are blogging platforms for older students, but younger students can simulate this experience with an app such as Seesaw that captures their voice or a video reflection and organizes them into a feed.

Reading responses that require children to think deeply about a topic often ask for students to take on the perspective of a reader. For example, students can create journal entries by taking on the perspective of a historical figure after reading primary source documents. Students can read their journal entries aloud and record their voices using a mobile app. Teachers can then create a video in which the audio recordings play while a picture of the historical figure appears on the screen.

Digital reading responses of any form should maintain high expectations for students. Introduce new options for a reading response by displaying a student exemplar or providing a checklist. Regardless of how students respond, they should be expected to use evidence from the text to support their thinking.

Promoting Deep Reading

Questions that promote deeper reading ask students to connect to the text directly. Students may lift a line or point to a paragraph as they support their thinking with evidence from the text. Deep-reading questions allow students to voice their opinions, make an inference, or evaluate an author's point of view while using text evidence to make an argument.

This framework is ideal for students to begin making connections between their current reading and other texts, themselves, or to the world in general. In order to do this, teachers must encourage students to move beyond the transparent (*What color was the mother's hair?*) and focus more on the inferential (*What motivated her to cut her hair?*).

Once students address questions that require them to support inferences with text evidence, connections begin to spark.

Asking Deeper Questions with Literary Texts

- What are some possible themes, and what evidence from the text guides you?
- What might the illustration tell you about the character's feelings?
- What may be making the character change her mind?
- Why might the author have made this decision?

Asking Deeper Questions with Informational Texts

- Does the author appear to be objective or biased? Why?
- What words or phrases has the author used to try to persuade you?
- What kind of research do you think the author may have needed to do to write this piece?

Developing Essential Questions

Students are able to read deeply when they can identify big ideas and connect these ideas to elements of their lives. No matter which texts are studied over the course of a school year, each lesson should come back to these overarching ideas:

Grades K–2

How can we see one of the author's big ideas by looking at the pictures?

- What do you think the book is about?
- How could you describe this character?
- If you could say one word about this story, what would it be?
- Can you act out this scene with feeling?

Grades 3–8

How do we recognize or determine the central idea (or theme) of a text?

- What central ideas are common across a variety of texts? How does the treatment of a particular central idea compare across a variety of texts?
- How do a character's qualities and actions contribute to the development of the central idea across the text?
- How is the central idea (or theme) explored and exemplified in both print and visual media?
- What are the essential ingredients of a scene?
- How can authors convey a particular idea within a scene?

Engaging students in literacy lessons forged by these questions will help them become not just competent, but thoughtful, self-motivated readers.

EdTech Spotlight

Reading Response Apps and Websites

There are a variety of technology tools that give students creative ways to respond to their reading and build excitement. Remember, it's important that you first plan the task and then search for an app that will meet your needs. Though many apps are "cool" and innovative, they are only useful if they are connected to your learning goals.

Here's a list of apps and websites you can use for reading responses.

- **ChatterPix Kids** (available on iOS devices): Students can snap a picture of their book and give a summary of what they've read.
- **Explain Everything**™ (available on iOS and Android devices): Students can narrate a time line of events from a section of their chapter book.
- **Spark Video** (available on the web or iOS devices): Students can create a book trailer using key details from the text.
- **PicCollage** (available on iOS and Android devices): After reading an informational text, students can combine details from the text with images they've found.
- **Storyboard That** (available on the web via any computer or tablet): Ask students to create a storyboard that shows an important part of the story they've read.
- **Tellagami** (available on iOS devices): Let students take on the role of a TV show host and pose questions to the main character.
- **Shadow Puppet Edu** (available on iOS devices): Ask students to snap a picture of five pages in their book where the illustrations helped them understand the story.
- **Canva** (available on the web and iOS devices): Students can respond to a reading-response prompt using this powerful graphic design tool.
- **Spark Page** (available on the web and iOS devices): Ask students to add their daily responses to their reading to a Spark Page.

Augmented and Virtual Reality

One of the most powerful things about technology is the ability to give both students and teachers access. This includes access to text, video, and interactive experiences, such as augmented reality (AR) and virtual reality (VR). AR and VR content often have clear connections to content-area instruction that can be used in English language arts lessons.

Augmented reality is a type of scannable technology. Students scan a special image with an AR app. Quiver is an example of an AR app in which teachers or caregivers print special coloring book pages from the Quiver website or app. Children color the page and then scan it with the Quiver app. The app turns their two-dimensional works of art into images that appear to be popping off the screen.

Augmented Reality Apps

- **Quiver**: coloring book pages with educational options
- **Star Walk Kids**: instant guide to constellations
- **Anatomy 4D**: see the human body pop off a page
- **Crayola® Color Alive**: coloring book pages

In the reading classroom, a teacher may use an AR app like Quiver to help students build background knowledge. Students can color a downloaded image of a volcano from the Quiver app or website and scan the page with their tablet. Watching the volcano pop off the screen can help students envision what happens during a volcanic eruption.

Augmented reality tools let students engage with content by seeing three-dimensional images layered on top of the real world. In the reading classroom, students may explore an informational text on the solar system. They can then use an augmented reality app like Star Walk Kids on a smartphone or a tablet to see where certain constellations appear in the sky. All they have to do is to open the Star Walk Kids app on their tablet or smartphone and hold their device toward the sky. These kinds of experiences help readers build background knowledge on a topic and apply new vocabulary in a real-world context.

Virtual reality is technology that simulates the real world. The most popular form of virtual reality is used with a headset. For example, Google Cardboard™ is a low-cost viewfinder through which students can look to see a smartphone screen in a totally new way. With virtual reality, students can be "transported" to new places, like a coral reef or a rainforest. In the reading classroom, students may look through a virtual reality viewfinder for a simulated visit to the Lincoln Memorial before reading a historical fiction novel about the Civil War.

Activity: Virtual Reality Prereading

Goal:

- Help students better understand the setting of a book and/or what life was like during a specific time period.

Preparation:

- Tailor a virtual reality prereading activity to the book you are reading and the technology you have available. In a low-tech classroom, this could mean exploring a 360-degree video with students on an interactive whiteboard. In a high-tech classroom, students can take turns using VR headsets with a smartphone.
- Choose the book you want to share with students, and identify important aspects of the setting, time period, and theme. This will help you figure out the best type of virtual reality experience to share with students.
- Locate a virtual reality video or simulation to share with students. Your choice will depend on your access to technology.

Steps for Success:

1. Share the virtual reality experience with students. This may be a whole class share on a projection screen or sharing of VR headsets among students.

2. After students have had an opportunity to experience virtual reality in action, ask them to share their wonderings and noticings with a partner. You may want to use the questions on the Virtual Reality Prereading sheets on page 166 and 167 as prompts for think-pair-shares.

3. Once students have had a chance to discuss their reactions to the virtual reality experience, question them about their noticings and wonderings. You will want to tailor these questions to the VR experiences of your students and the connections you would like them to make to the new book.

4. As you read the new book to students, pause to make connections to the VR experience where notable. Students can reflect on how the VR prereading experience helped them make meaning of the text.

EdTech Spotlight

Google Cardboard

Have you tried Google Cardboard in your classroom? This incredibly affordable (under $10!) tool lets students explore virtual reality straight from your classroom. You can take your students on virtual field trips, help them understand life in different parts of the world, and push students to ask questions about the world around them.

When virtual reality first came on the stage, it seemed as if the cost would make it impossible for teachers to use it as a learning tool. The combination of a Google Cardboard viewer and a mobile device makes this the perfect choice for classroom teachers. The handful of quality apps mentioned below are great choices for teachers looking to combine the Google Cardboard with apps developed for both iPhones® and Android™ devices.

Apps to Use with Google Cardboard

YouVisit takes students on virtual college tours. A virtual reality college tour is a great choice for students who might not be able to visit all of the colleges to which they plan to apply.

Nearpod can help students experience the world through engaging lessons and virtual field trips to faraway places.

ThingLink provides VR experiences that can transport students to ecosystems around the world. Lessons can be accessed from the mobile app.

NYT VR is an easy-to-use app with dynamic content from the *New York Times*. This free app for iOS and Android devices let viewers experience the sights and sounds of places around the world.

Discovery VR is loaded with lots of great content. There are adventure experiences, like deep-sea diving, mountain biking, and the opportunity to see endangered species in action. If you or your students are fans of Discovery Channel programming, you'll love the content from shows like *MythBusters* and *Survivorman*.

Dear Families,   _____

Let's make sure all of our children love to read deeply! Children who are active, thoughtful readers reread books they love, ask questions, and read to gain a better understanding of the text. They are doing this because they care about what they read and feel passionately about these thoughts. Please make sure to create a safe space for your children to read at home and explore ways to help them feel comfortable rereading books and conversing about their thoughts and wonderings. Create a cozy corner with a tablet and/or a range of fun books for your children to experience. Put books and magazines in surprising places, especially books they've already read, so they can browse again. Reading deeply means we get to reread our favorite books.

In your home, take a moment to sit with your child for a *deep dive* as a reader. Select a chapter book or a piece of informational text to explore together. Share your own noticings. Maybe the setting reminds you of a favorite movie, or a character acts just like someone you know. Carve out time to talk about what you've read, not just the *who* and *where*, but how you personally connect and react to the text. When your child shares his or her thoughts or feelings with you, be a good listener. Let your child focus on how the book affects his or her life. Some questions you can ask are:

- Why do you love this book?

- What more do you want to read by this author?

- Would you like to reread this text with me?

- What are you wondering about?

Thank you for your support in building the Five Habits! Let's keep going!

With appreciation,

Queridas familias:

¡Asegurémonos de que a todos nuestros hijos les encanta leer a profundidad! Los niños que son lectores activos y atentos releen los libros que les encantan, hacen preguntas y leen para entender mejor el texto. Hacen esto porque les importa lo que leen y les apasiona lo que piensan, Por favor, asegúrense de crear en casa un espacio seguro en donde sus hijos puedan leer, y busquen maneras útiles para que se sientan con la confianza de releer libros y conversar acerca de sus pensamientos y sus preguntas. Crean un rinconcito íntimo con una tableta y/o una variedad de libros divertidos para su hijo. Coloquen libros y revistas en lugares inesperados especialmente los libros que sus hijos ya han leído para que puedan darles una hojeada nuevamente. Releer nuestros libros favoritos es parte de leer a profundidad.

Tomen un momento en casa para sentarse con su hijo y zambullirse en la lectura. Escojan juntos un libro con capítulos o un texto informativo. Cuéntele sus propios pensamientos. Tal vez el escenario le recuerde a su película favorita, o quizá un personaje se comporta exactamente como alguien que usted conoce. Designe un tiempo para conversar acerca de lo que han leído. No tan solo el "quién" o el "dónde" del texto, sino también cómo usted se identifica con el texto y cómo reacciona ante él. Cuando su hijo le cuente sus pensamientos o sentimientos, escuche con atención. Deje que su hijo se enfoque en cómo el libro afecta a su vida. Algunas preguntas que podría hacer son:

- ¿Por qué te encanta este libro?

- ¿Qué más de este autor te gustaría leer?

- ¿Te gustaría releer este texto conmigo?

- ¿Qué más te gustaría saber?

¡Gracias por su apoyo en desarrollar los Cinco hábitos [Five Habits]! ¡Sigamos adelante!

Con agradecimiento,

Reading Closely

Jeremy loves how the punctuation in the poem he is reading makes it possible to read fast and sound musical. Emma wonders about why her science text contains certain transition words that repeat frequently. Carlos loves a line in the sports article he is reading and pulls it out to carefully study it. He wants to write like that! With reading, we tend to assume kids want to move quickly. But Jeremy, Emma, and Carlos are making meaning of their texts through close examination. They look at the tiniest detail, the author's word choice, or the white space between the stanzas. All of these clues help active readers piece together a bigger picture. In reading closely, they have uncovered an understanding of the text that will inspire a curiosity and love of learning. This is reading closely.

Close reading is the act of making reading visible. It is unpacking a text by pausing, rereading, and jotting notes in the margins. It is taking time to move through a passage, pointing out details that may otherwise go unnoticed. Close reading should feel fulfilling, like solving the answer to a riddle by deconstructing everything from the white space, to a sentence, to a paragraph, to a theme.

This chapter will discuss how to help students access complex text through close reading by leveraging technology tools to build foundational reading experiences. Digital tools can energize traditional teaching and give students new ways to read text closely. Close reading is an essential component of taming the wild text, and technology tools can support students on this journey.

For English language learners, close reading of text can be very challenging but also quite thrilling, as it gives students the chance to both practice English skills and master the complex text. For close reading, English language learners should practice their skills primarily in English-based text. This has the twofold effect of increasing English-based language skills and introducing students to a skill they will need throughout the rest of their academic experience. Having English language learners identify a poet's reasons for using white space or determining why a writer used a specific word are both very sophisticated tasks. English language learners can do it. It's so exciting to realize that the language of the text can be tamed when we slow down a reading instead of speeding it up!

For below-level learners, close reading can be done with simpler texts. Teachers must occasionally model texts at different complexity levels for the whole class so that below level learners do not feel marginalized. For example, a deceptively simple picture book such as *Goodnight, Moon* can provide a great close-reading lesson. Margaret Wise Brown was a master of writing texts that use simple words but convey big ideas. Using these simpler texts to demonstrate a close-reading lesson helps students of all levels feel involved and engaged.

Appreciating Text Complexity

Imagine a staircase with an endless series of landings where children can pause to revel in thoughtfully selected core and independent texts. This is the model in which 21st century education standards were built: a graceful, systemic ascent in grade level text complexity. In order to prepare children for this climb, to make them feel exhilarated rather than depleted by the journey, teachers must equip them with appropriate scaffolding for their primary task: reading to make meaning. The ultimate purpose of the staircase model of complexity is to cultivate readers who are experts by the time they graduate. So, whether their college close reading is a piece of timeless literature or the text of a math problem, they approach the page free of fear.

But what is the appropriate scaffolding for such a journey? The first step is recognizing every student's right to quality text that ranges in complexity level. Even the simplest text will help a child read more closely. While more complex texts allow students to confront comprehension obstacles that put close-reading tools to use, the difficulty of the text itself is not what helps us master close reading. It is having a child feel confident and powerful enough to investigate texts like a detective.

There are a number of ways in which teachers can determine a text's complexity. Many schools have adopted student leveling systems, such as Lexile®, Guided Reading, or Developmental Reading Assessment (DRA). With these systems, students are assessed and receive a suggested "level." Texts are also assessed using qualitative methods, quantitative methods, or a mix of both. Comparing the texts' levels with students' levels helps teachers anticipate the amount of challenge a text will present to each student. Parents, teachers, and students can use this information to search for books that present the appropriate level of complexity for the individual reader and task. While reading levels offer a place to start, the Core Principals for Text Complexity must still be considered for each student.

Core Principles for Text Complexity

Over the years, school districts and state departments have defined complexity of text in the following three ways: **Quantitative Measures, Qualitative Measures,** and **Reader and Task Considerations.**

Quantitative

Quantitative features of text relate to decoding and fluency skills, including sight-word vocabulary, decoding unfamiliar words, recognizing simple and complex sentence structures, and increasing fluency.

Qualitative

Qualitative features of text relate to comprehension. The levels of meaning and purpose, structure, language conventions and clarity, and the knowledge demands of a text all affect its level of complexity.

Considering Reader and Task

This includes the specific tasks that are required for a reader to access the texts they are reading. Readers who understand the particular genre can attack a text more successfully. Readers with some background knowledge about the content can uncover the messages in a text.

Teachers should be mindful of a tendency to give too much weight to the quantitative element in identifying what is "complex." This type of criterion forms the basis of most of the dialogue around text bands and grade level recommended text, so it is important to remember that the determination of text complexity involves a combination of variables. Meaning, theme, irony, subtlety, and all of the other qualitative elements cannot be measured scientifically but are equally as important. Remember: literacy and the art of language are just that—artful.

A Balanced Approach to Reading Instruction

Younger students are learning to decode, comprehend, and build stamina all at once, so it may be advantageous to encourage students to read an "easier" book. This way, students can build stamina or dig into metaphors or punctuation use without tripping over unfamiliar or "frustration-level" vocabulary.

With this balanced approach in mind, teachers can use **read alouds, shared reading, small-group reading instruction,** and **independent reading** to provide students with instructional reading experiences in challenging texts:

- During a **read aloud**, demonstrate and model close reading of complex text to meaningfully interact with grade level and above grade level texts.

- **Shared reading** allows teachers to use the text instructionally and to reinforce learning with continued practice or rereading of a text. Collaborative discussion of the shared text or parallel practice in a related text are important components of shared reading.

- The proven power of systematically scheduled **small-group reading instruction** provides students with differentiated instruction in a more accountable, intimate learning environment. Here, the focus can be on both the quantitative and qualitative challenges awaiting students in the texts.

- And of course, having students **read independently** for at least 20 minutes or more each day is the key to all close reading. It is during this time that students practice the work of close reading in books of their choice.

Activity: Close Reading for Multiple Perspectives

Goals:

- Students will support their thinking and conclusions through text evidence.
- Students will combine their voice and understanding of a text using multimedia.

Steps for Success:

1. Ask students to choose a character from the book they are reading. You may decide to have students pick a historical figure or notable person they've read about in a piece of informational text.

2. Provide a direction for students as they prepare to take on the role of their character. You may say, "Imagine you are [character]. What would she write in a letter to a friend when she describes new challenges in her life?" or "Imagine your are [character]. What would he say if he was asked for his opinion about [current event]?"

3. Independently or in pairs, students can brainstorm what their character would say in the situation you've presented.

4. Have students write their response using specific evidence from the text. You may want them to call out page numbers or paragraphs as they write.

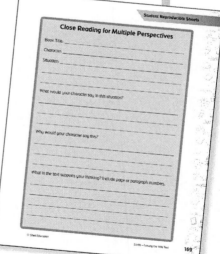

5. Using a tool that requires students to record their voice or narrate a video or slideshow, have students read their writing aloud. If students were asked to cite page or paragraph numbers in their writing, they can omit them from their recording.

6. Once students have recorded their videos, they can share them with peers or another audience you've found for them.

Demonstrating Close-Reading Proficiency

Students should be included when planning close-reading protocols and setting goals. Students can discuss how they want to approach the text, allowing them to build on previous work in order to get to the next level. Here is one example:

Level One	Preview by examining the overall form and features of the text.
Level Two	Read for *what* the text says. Try to summarize what the text is mainly about. Clarify unknown words.
Level Three	Read for *how* the text is written. Analyze the author's choices of structure, words, and phrases to deepen your understanding of the text.
Level Four	Read for *why* the text is written. Determine the purpose and central ideas of the text.

Independent Reading Tips

- Feature a "Close Read of the Week" on Google Docs where everyone can comment on the text together.

- Invite students to bring in surprising texts to study: recipes, emails, social-media posts, infographics, magazine articles, etc.

- Have one-on-one conversations with students to explore their thinking and conclusions about a text. Support and encourage use of text evidence as they explain their thinking.

Questions for Close Reading in Fiction Texts

- What central idea(s) are being addressed in this text? What textual evidence can you provide to support this claim?

- What events in the story are most closely related to the theme? What evidence do you see in the sentences?

- How does the main character change across the story? Can you find a location in the text that shows it?

- What do we learn about this character from what he or she says? Use a quotation in your explanation.

- What characteristics describe this character? What text evidence backs up your thinking?

- What have you noticed about the character's relationships with other characters? How are these relationships important to the story?

- How is the setting important to the story?

- How does the problem in the story get solved?

- What does the sentence structure tell us about this character's feelings?

- What does the white space do to impact your impression of this part of the story?

Questions for Close Reading in Nonfiction Texts

- What is the purpose of this text?

- How is the text structured? How does the structure support the reader?

- What in the text is factual? What is an interpretation? An opinion?

- Does the author use technical, connotative, or figurative language? Cite examples. How does this language affect meaning and tone?

- Does the author make use of analogies?

- What are the central ideas of the text?

- How does the author support the central idea with evidence? Is the evidence relevant and sufficient?

- What is the author's point of view? Show some sentences that demonstrate it.

- What are the author's credentials? Do they make him or her credible as a writer on this topic?

- How do the white space and bolded words affect the meaning of this text?

- If you look at the photos or pictures, what do you think the author is trying to convey?

Questions for Close Reading in Persuasive Texts

- What claim is the author making? What would be the counterclaim?
- Who is the target audience?
- Is the reasoning in the argument sound? Share evidence.
- How strong is the evidence that supports the claim?
- How does the author refute the counterclaim?
- Who or what influences this author's point of view?
- Is some evidence emphasized more than other evidence?
- Is some evidence purposefully omitted or de-emphasized?
- What questions do you still have after listening to both sides?
- Were you persuaded? Why? Why not?
- What is your opinion about the issue, and why?
- How does the author use punctuation to highlight his or her opinion?
- What do the lead and ending sentences do for the author's point of view?

Annotating Text

The purpose of annotating text can vary depending on goals for interacting with a particular passage or excerpt. Students may start the year practicing how to underline key details that support the author's argument and then learn to use additional annotations, like recording a question in the margin. Teachers can introduce annotation to students by providing common structures. With practice, students will develop independent reading behaviors to apply outside the classroom.

Many classrooms have a set routine for annotating text. All students may circle a new or an important vocabulary word or put a star next to an example of author bias. Setting up structures for annotating text can help students stay focused. They can share their thinking with fellow readers as they show off their annotations or tackle a new text together. If teachers are going to have students follow a set structure for coding a text, it can be useful to check in with colleagues in earlier grades as well as at their own grade level. Having a consistent routine for coding can help students focus more energy on the material in front of them and less on remembering the established coding marks.

Digital tools make it easy for students of any age to annotate a text. Students have the option to access a text online, upload a text saved to a device, or snap a picture of a print text they would like to annotate. Annotation tools let students highlight, color-code, add text, and record their voice. The tools teachers choose to use will vary depending on the devices they have access to and the age level of their students. In an early elementary reading classroom, students may snap a picture of a page in a picture book with their tablets and circle the part of the picture that supports their thinking. Older students may open up a PDF version of an informational text passage and annotate it in on their mobile device. With technology tools, students can write on text or record their thinking with a few taps on the screen.

Annotation Tools for Students

- Kami
- iAnnotate
- iTunes U®
- Nearpod

Activity: Introducing Annotations on Digital Devices

Goal:

- Students will learn a set of routines and markup strategies for interacting with digital text.

Preparation:

- Decide which digital annotation tool to use with students. It should be something that meets instructional goals, like using color-coding options or recording voice notes.
- Have three or four students become "expert users" by exploring the tool during a free period. This can take some of the burden off introducing a new tool by giving students another set of people to direct their questions to.

Steps for Success:

1. Model use of the tool in an authentic context. If you've already set expectations for annotation, like underlining a new word or circling a sentence that made you wonder, these structures can be transferred to this digital work.

2. Give students time to practice the work flow of opening a reading passage with an annotation tool. You may start off by giving them a passage that is at or below their instructional level to emphasize practicing annotation.

Note: This interaction with text will vary by grade level. You may find that your students in second grade use their finger to highlight new words on their tablet, while older students use a textbox to add a thought about their reading.

Graphic Organizers and Concept Maps

Graphic organizers give teachers the power to model explicitly how they want students to interact with a text while practicing skills like sequencing events or comparing two ideas. Graphic organizers help students categorize ideas, make connections, and pull evidence from the text. Armed with organized information, students are more prepared to respond to a prompt about a text.

Technology Tip

If you have a favorite graphic organizer you've always used on paper, save the document as a PDF instead of printing it. Students can open the PDF on their tablet or computer to annotate the page.

Although teachers may introduce Venn diagrams and T-charts to students, interactive mapping tools provide students with the flexibility to organize their thinking in a way that makes sense to them. Whether choosing print or digital tools, it is essential that students see teachers model as they think aloud. By doing so, students will have a better understanding of how to interact with a text during a close read.

Teachers can ensure that each student has access to graphic organizers on his or her tablet. Students can then use an annotation app to record thoughts and information directly onto the graphic organizers. This can be especially beneficial if students are primarily reading paperback books. They can keep their books by their sides as they fill in graphic organizers on their tablets.

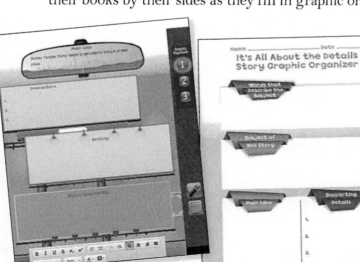

Concept maps, sometimes called mind maps, give students space to create their own representation of their thoughts. With a concept map, students start with an idea or topic in the center and gradually build out as they uncover more information. Students can read a book, such as *Because of Winn-Dixie*, and search for examples of a theme, like *belonging*. They can put their topic, *belonging*, in the center and draw lines out from the center as they jot down examples of belonging they've found in the text. If any of these events are related, students can connect the ideas on their map.

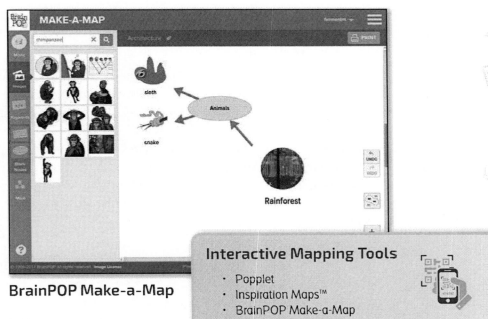

BrainPOP Make-a-Map

Interactive Mapping Tools

- Popplet
- Inspiration Maps™
- BrainPOP Make-a-Map

Digital Anchor Charts

Anchor charts can often be found hanging on classroom walls, acting as a visual reminder of concepts that have been taught. There are anchor charts that remain up throughout the school year and some that are only referenced during a particular unit of study. Teachers have different strategies for making anchor charts easy for students to utilize.

When teaching a mini-lesson or introducing a new concept, anchor charts are often used to remind students of big ideas or concepts that they need to remember. Anchor charts are often called reference charts because students use these charts to help them when they are independently practicing a concept.

Throughout a unit of study, teachers can end up with dozens of these anchor charts but not enough wall space to hold them all!

In a tech-friendly classroom, though, teachers have a variety of options for making charts easily accessible to students. First, picture taking matters—a lot. Teachers should take pictures of student work to use as exemplars for next year's unit. They can take pictures of great things they see in other teachers' classrooms or anchor charts that worked well and should be replicated the following year. With a smartphone in hand, teachers can capture student learning and ideas to take back to their everyday practice. However, taking pictures of anchor charts can have an instant impact on student learning.

Technology tools make it possible to capture anchor charts through the school year and make them accessible to students on their digital devices. Imagine a room full of anchor charts that provide useful information to students. Snap a picture of an anchor chart in a classroom, or take a screenshot of the information projected on an interactive whiteboard. These pictures can be placed in a digital space for all students to see, like a shared folder in Google Drive™, or tagged with keywords in a learning-management system. Pictures of anchor charts can also be added to an iBooks® library. When loaded onto an iPad, students can open up iBooks and see collections of reference charts from previous units.

In a classroom with more technology in use, chart papers may have been replaced with an interactive whiteboard. This digital tool makes it easier to model certain concepts and lets teachers easily pull up a blank page, a passage, or a large picture onto the screen. Interactive whiteboards and document cameras are often used to model best practices for students instead of hanging up chart paper in the classroom.

Tools for Creating Digital Anchor Charts

- Adobe Spark Post
- Canva
- Keynote®

Activity: Digital Anchor Charts

Goal:

- Students will learn how to make the most of digital anchor charts.

Preparation:

- Pick and choose which resources will help students, and decide how to organize them in a way that isn't too overwhelming.

- Decide how you will capture and organize anchor charts and snapshots from digital lessons. You may choose to create a shared folder on a service like Dropbox or dedicate a section in a learning management system for these resources.

Steps for Success:

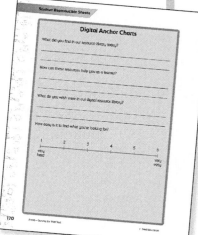

1. Model how to access the resources now stored online and accessible on their devices. Take them through the steps of locating a reference chart or a collection of resources.

2. Give students a chance to explore the digital anchor chart library you've created. You may want to ask them to locate a particular resource, as in a scavenger hunt, or give them more freedom to explore.

3. After your students have had a chance to check out the digital collection of anchor charts, ask for their feedback on ease of use, and listen to their responses to see if there are ways you could make this process even easier for them.

Close-reading activities can happen with a variety of text, including images, news articles, or a single page from a high-quality chapter book. Regardless of the text, students should be able to pull evidence to support their thinking. Children of all ages should get in the habit of this, as they can no longer rely solely on personal connections or prior experiences. Making connections to previous reading or life experiences is a great way to get students excited about text, but moving beyond this practice involves reading closely. Even when there is no one right answer, students should be able to point to a picture or quote a passage in a text to support their thinking about what they have read. Teachers must provide texts that inspire and connect to students. They must empower students to make the choices for whole class close-reading lessons so that they are using all kinds of texts to show the power of close reading.

Dear Families, _____

    Children who read closely take time to linger and look carefully at everything, from pictures to words to sentences. Close readers discuss the motivation of authors, and they think about why they chose to include a particular word or sentence in their writing. We want our children to read so closely that they can share a thought about the text that mentions a phrase, a sentence, or a single word. Invite your kids to wonder aloud why an author chose to describe a character by using a particular word or why a science writer chose a particular photo.

    In your home, take a moment to reread a favorite book or magazine article with your child. Ask him or her to pause to look at a picture, a sentence, or a word. Discuss why a sentence or paragraph makes you feel a certain way about what you have read. Questions you could ask include:

- Why do you think the author chose to use that word?

- Why do you think the author used those punctuation marks there?

- What do you like about this sentence?

- What themes do you notice, and where do you see them in your book?

    Keep the noticings on your tablet in a folder that you and your child can look at again and again as an unfolding of their development as readers.

    Thank you for helping us on our journey of the Five Habits!

With Appreciation,

Dear Families, _____

Los niños que leen atentamente toman el tiempo para detenerse y observar todo cuidadosamente, desde los dibujos hasta las palabras y las oraciones. Los lectores meticulosos hablan sobre los motivos de un autor y piensan en por qué un autor eligió incluir en su escritura una palabra o una oración específica. Queremos que nuestros hijos lean tan atentamente que puedan contar un pensamiento acerca del texto que contenga una frase, una oración o una palabra específica del texto. Anime a sus hijos a pensar en voz alta sobre por qué un autor eligió describir a un personaje usando una palabra en particular, o por qué eligió un escritor de ciencias una fotografía específica.

Tomen un momento en casa para releer con su hijo su libro preferido o un artículo de revista. Pídanle que tome una pausa para observar un dibujo, una oración o una palabra. Hablen sobre por qué una oración o un párrafo les hacen sentir de cierta manera sobre lo que acaban de leer. Algunas preguntas que pueden hacer son:

- ¿Por qué crees que el autor eligió usar esa palabra?

- ¿Por qué crees que el autor usó esos signos de puntuación?

- ¿Qué te gusta de esta oración?

- ¿Qué temas puedes observar y dónde los encuentras en el libro?

Guarde las anotaciones en su tableta en una carpeta que usted y su hijo puedan ver una y otra vez para observar el desarrollo de su hijo como lector.

¡Gracias por ayudarnos en el camino hacia los Cinco hábitos [Five Habits]!

Con agradecimiento,

Reading Socially

Rayna is looking forward to her upcoming reading celebration. She is revisiting her favorite books from throughout the year and recording favorite parts on an online document. Sammy is wild for a new series he has recently discovered. He is going to make a book trailer to make sure his friends will also read these books. He is also going to create a series of tweets so other grade-level friends can hear the news of these books. Shin is eager to talk with his best friend about a collection of books on art that they have found together. They make a plan to talk about it and then do an art project that is based on the style they are reading about. This is reading socially.

Establishing an authentic audience for student creations is essential. Students should know that their work is being viewed by real people in a true context. Deciding on an authentic audience for student work at the beginning of a unit or before kicking off a project can set a purpose for learning. If students know that their reading responses will be posted on a blog for their families to visit, their sense of purpose grows. If teachers give students the chance to tweet their favorite part of a read-aloud to the author of a book, their sense of purpose grows. If students can celebrate their reading accomplishments, their sense of purpose grows. In this way, they can tame the wild text by setting a purposeful plan for sharing their reading experiences.

For English language learners, reading socially is a crucial part of their reading development. Educators sometimes focus so intensively on the grammatical structures of texts that they forget how important it is to publically acknowledge a student's progress. Having a weekly reading celebration gives students the feeling of belonging to the larger community. Also, the idea of reading socially and using technology to do so is a relief for students who dread the five-paragraph essay. Reading with the purpose of sharing a tweet about a part of the book that moves them is not only fun to do but it's also short. English language learners can practice their English skills without tedium.

For below-level learners, celebration is vital. Purpose is essential. So often, they are pulled out for remediation and are not in the classroom when joy is the most present. This must change. Reading socially must be something in which students are fully engaged. A simple, colorful drawing representing a favorite passage hung up in the hallway or their presence at a reading celebration is going to bring so much joy. And that joy translates to wanting to read more and more. In the day of a teacher, minutes count. The more that below-level learners read, and want to read the more progress they will make.

Technology tools make it easier to connect with authentic audiences, and strengthening relationships with community stakeholders is an important part of this process. Classes may decide to Skype™ with a local or faraway farm to share new knowledge after reading an informational text featuring roosters or cows. The PTA president who manages the school Facebook page may post a picture of student reading projects to share with the community. With technology, teachers can share student work quickly with a few taps of the screen.

Authentic Responses to Reading

Readers who explore text can respond to what they've read through a range of activities that feel purposeful in the world of a reading community. Learners are becoming increasingly accustomed to sharing their thinking with a large audience thanks to the proliferation of social-media tools. Students should have opportunities to respond to reading in an authentic manner.

Book Trailers

Book trailers require students to respond with a critical eye and for an authentic audience, thinking deeply about what they've read and using evidence from the text to support their thinking. A book trailer is a videographic way of describing one's positive thoughts about a book they've read. Usually lasting no more than two minutes, a book trailer is designed as an advertisement to encourage others to read a specific book. The audience will rely on book trailers to guide them toward their next book, and this authentic response to reading can have a huge impact on the student's community of readers.

Tools for Creating a Book Trailer

- **Spark Video**: combine images, icons and voice
- **iMovie**: trailer templates make it easy to get started
- **Shadow Puppet Edu**: incorporates narration over a series of still images

Activity: Book Trailer

Goals:

- Students will share specific information from the text as they provide a synopsis of the book and strategically highlight different aspects of the contents.

Preparation:

- Decide whether this will be an individual activity or something that students complete in partnerships or with a literature circle.
- Prepare copies (print or digital) of the Book Trailer Brainstorming Sheet (page 171) and/or Book Trailer Storyboard Template (page 172).

Steps for Success:

1. As students get ready to start a new book or are about to finish a text, introduce the concept of a book trailer. You will want to find examples that mirror your expectations or create your own exemplar.

2. Share your expectations with students including an explanation of who will view their trailers. This audience could include members of their own class, other students in the school, or an audience reached with social media.

3. Share graphic organizers with students that will help them plan for their book trailer. The Book Trailer Brainstorming Sheet on page 171 and Book Trailer Storyboard Template found on page 172 can help students organize their ideas.

4. Once students have developed their plan, introduce them to the technology tool they will use to make their book trailer. Depending on the experience students have, you may give them a few options to choose from.

5. Provide time for students to create their book trailer. Students may want to use headphones to record audio or find a quiet space in the classroom.

6. After students have finished their book trailers, share their creations with the audience you've chosen.

Shelfies

Students should feel proud when they finish a book. They can share their accomplishments by snapping a picture of a book cover. When a student holds the book, poses with it, and takes these snapshots himself or herself, they're popularly called *shelfies*. Although we didn't come up with this term, we love the idea of placing a twist on the selfie craze!

Students can take a shelfie with a new book or a book they just finished. They could add a caption or hashtag to their photo, respond to a reading prompt, or write a short recommendation for a fellow reader. Teachers may also ask students to create a list of resources that classmates could use to learn more about the setting of a book or the information presented. If they make this list using an online tool like Google Docs, they can link their document to a QR Code. Teachers can place the QR code on the front of the physical book, and classmates can scan it for instant information. Tech-friendly activities like these set a purpose for reading (sharing an opinion, collecting useful resources) while giving students an opportunity to explore digital tools.

EdTech Spotlight

Shelfie Book Recommendations

- Have students make their shelfie talk by snapping a picture of their favorite book and opening the image in an app, like ChatterPix Kids. Here they can slice a mouth across an image and record their voice to create a talking movie.

- Ask students to snap their shelfie and compile a collection of their pictures in an app like Spark Video. They can record a short recommendation for their book, and their voice recording will play over their shelfie. Collect these from students, and create a class movie of favorite books.

- Students can use an app like Explain Everything™ to import pictures and add captions to shelfies. Kids can annotate an image and use text (or audio) to record their recommendation.

- Create shelfie posters and add a QR code to take interested readers to information about where they can find the book in the school library. A QR code could also connect users to an audio book recommendation.

Activity: Shelfie Book Recommendation

Goal:

- Students will turn a shelfie into a book recommendation.

Preparation:

- Compile examples of shelfies you've taken or found on social media.

Steps for Success:

1. Introduce the idea of a shelfie to students. Share examples.

2. After students have finished reading a book, set up a protocol for how they will go about taking a shelfie. This will vary depending on how many devices your students have access to and the workflow in your classroom.

3. Once students have snapped their shelfie, you can introduce how you'd like them to respond to the book. You may ask them to add a hashtag, a comment, a favorite quote from the book, or a longer recommendation. Be sure to set expectations and share exemplars of finished products.

4. Once students have completed their shelfies, display their pictures on a bulletin board, post their pictures on an online forum or social media (with permission), or create a slide show to play in the library.

Backchannels

A backchannel is a space for students to share their thoughts and view the thinking of their peers in real time. Before introducing a new book, students should partner up in front of a shared screen. This means they are both seated in front of one tablet. A tool like TodaysMeet provides a space for students to share their thinking before, during, and after a read aloud.

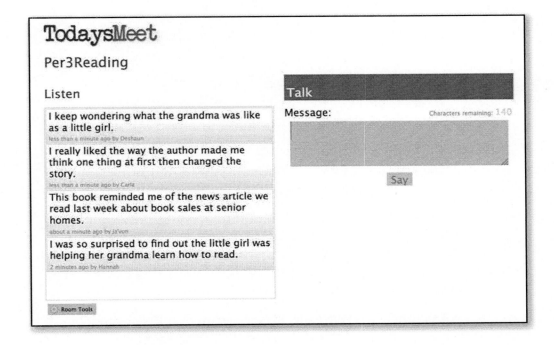

Backchannels in Action

We recently had the opportunity to work with teachers in North Carolina on behalf of the awesome folks at LitLife. The teachers at this school were definitely excited to introduce technology tools into their everyday lessons. One of the tips we shared with teachers is the power of a backchannel during literacy instruction, especially if you have only a handful of devices for students.

EdTech Spotlight

Create a Read Aloud Backchannel in Your Classroom

Start students off by having them open up your TodaysMeet backchannel on their shared device. You can ask students a question like:

- What do you think this book will be about based on the illustrations you see on the cover?
- Given what we know about this author, why might he write a book about _____?

Before they type in their answer, ask students to think-pair-share or turn-and-talk to their partners. Then, they can decide on one response and type it into their shared backchannel response.

When you're ready to jump into the book, you can have students tilt their tablet screen to a 45-degree angle, so they can focus on the text as you read aloud. You can stop periodically to pose questions as student pairs follow the same procedure as above.

As students respond to the questions you pose during a read aloud, you can listen in to their discussions as you circulate around the room. At the end of the lesson, you'll have the backchannel to review to see all of the responses from partners in your classroom.

This read aloud activity is the perfect way to cultivate digital citizenship skills, gather formative assessment data, and increase participation during literacy instruction.

Try this activity with one of our favorite read aloud books:

- *Those Shoes* by Maribeth Boelts
- *Pink and Say* by Patricia Polacco
- *Train to Somewhere* by Eve Bunting

Social Media

An exploration of social-media sharing can help students form and evaluate social-media partnerships. Teachers may ask students to spend the first few minutes of class searching for and then reading short articles located on a website like Newsela. Students can share an article they've found on a social-sharing site for their class. Perhaps fourth graders will find an article, write one sentence describing why it's a great read, and post it on a collaborative online space like Padlet. Students should also have time to look over the contributions of their classmates and choose a new article to read. Students will begin to develop reading partnerships by identifying which classmates share similar interests with them.

Hashtags

A hashtag, popular on Twitter, Facebook®, or Instagram®, is a hash mark or pound sign (#) followed by a keyword. A hashtag is used to keep online information organized into different categories. For example, if a student loves the picture book *I Dissent: Ruth Bader Ginsburg Makes Her Mark* by Debbie Levy, he may snap a picture of the book or share his favorite part in a Facebook post with "#readaloud" or "#biography." People who see his post can click on the hashtag and view other posts containing the same hashtag. Social media apps like Twitter, Facebook, or Instagram include search features, allowing users to see what other people are saying about a particular topic. If teachers are looking for new ideas to bring back to the classroom, searching a hashtag like #edtech (for education technology) or #ipaded (iPads in education) can help locate information on these respective topics.

Activity: Hashtag Reading Response

Goals:

- Students will model their reading responses after social media writing.
- Students can use hashtags as a way to organize their thinking and categorize their reading responses.

Preparation:

- Compile examples of tweets you've written or found on social media.

Steps for Success:

1. Explain that hashtags help people organize their thinking around a big idea. A hashtag makes it easier to search for big ideas, like #readaloud or #4thgradebooks. Here are a few examples you can use as a model:

   - *Because of Winn-Dixie* makes my heart smile because it shows the power of friendship. #realisticfiction #fourstars #friendship
   - *The Evolution of Calpurnia Tate* reminds me why it is important to stay true to your beliefs. #historicalfiction #courage

2. Ask students to pause when they are finished reading a picture book or a passage in a chapter book and write a response. Using a list you've created or the class has brainstormed, have students add two or three hashtags that connect their response to a larger category.

3. After students have responded to their reading with a hashtag, ask them to share with the class. Encourage them to find similarities among their reading choices and reading experiences.

Tweeting

A tweet is a 140-character public statement. In the classroom, it can be a model for a short response to reading. Tweeting gives all students a space to respond to reading, and a limit for their response. Students can count characters or simply limit their response to one or two sentences.

In one instance, *The Book with No Pictures* by B. J. Novak was read aloud to a group of children. As the students laughed along with the pages, Monica snapped a picture and posted it to Twitter. She included the author's Twitter handle in the tweet as a virtual shout-out to the author. (Doing so also helps Monica's online followers to easily locate more information about his work.) A few days later, Monica's phone lit up with a notification. B. J. Novak had replied to the tweet! The next week, Monica was able to share the reply from author B. J. Novak with the group of children, who were thrilled!

The idea of tweeting to authors is not a novel concept. Teachers around the world use Twitter to connect with their students' favorite authors. Although one may not initially think of a children's author as a reading partner, these relationships can be critical to student success. Authors often respond to tweets, Skype with classrooms, and answer emails. Whether a favorite author chooses to answer becomes less important when teachers are focused on building the capacity of readers to understand channels of communication and the possibilities that abound.

Activity: Tweeting the Read Aloud

Goal:

- Students will use Twitter to respond to an event, a television show, or an article they've read.

Preparation:

- The way you implement this activity will vary depending on grade level and classroom culture. Set up your own class Twitter account, and tweet student thinking to provide an authentic audience.

- Choose a book to share with students and a prompt you would like to discuss when you finish reading the book. The prompt could be as simple as *Would you recommend this book to a friend? Why or why not?* or as specific as *How does this book connect to another text we've explored this year?*

Steps for Success:

1. Distribute an index card, or ask students to open a digital exit slip on their devices.

2. Explain to students that their responses should be short and powerful. You may show them an example of a Twitter feed from a news organization, an author, or a notable figure.

3. Have students complete their responses, and provide time for them to share with a partner, a small group, or the whole class. You may decide to take a few student responses and post them to a class Twitter feed.

4. If you post these short responses on Twitter, tag the author of the text you read. You can find the Twitter handle for this person by typing his or her name in Twitter's search bar or visiting his or her website.

Option: If your younger students respond to reading with illustrations, snap pictures of their illustrations and post them on your class Twitter feed. Make sure to share this authentic audience with students and celebrate how the world can now view their work.

EdTech Spotlight

Eight Ways to Get Every Student Tweeting

There are lots of ways to incorporate this social media platform into your classroom. Older students may have their own Twitter account and post reflections to class discussions online. Younger students can participate in Twitter-inspired activities or contribute ideas to their class Twitter feed. Here are eight ways to get every student tweeting:

1. Introduce hashtags as a way to categorize learning. Create hashtags with your class that go along with an activity like categorizing books by genres or strategies to solve a math problem.

2. Ask students to tweet their big takeaways from the day's lesson at the end of class. Some students may post their Twitter-inspired exit slip on a class board, while others may head straight to Twitter and include your class hashtag on their post.

3. Tweet your students' work, including creations posted online or snapshots of student projects. Remember to make sure you have permission to share student work and images online.

4. Ask students to write a paper/pencil synopsis of a book, or identify a key argument in a text using only 140 characters. You may choose to share their writing on your class Twitter feed.

5. Ask students to create a tweetable image using Spark Post. Students can use this creation tool to capture a favorite quote or a lingering question about a topic.

6. Next time your students attend an assembly or watch a video in class, set up a backchannel. Similar to the tweeting that takes place during a live sporting event or television show, comments can be in real time.

7. Have students create a make-believe Twitter profile for a character from a book or a figure from history. Students can simulate a conversation between two characters in classic literature or one between a past president and a contemporary figure.

8. Hashtags are often used to spark a conversation. Choose a relevant hashtag like #HerStoryCampaign, and have students generate tweets you can post to a class account.

Connecting Globally

Social media tools help readers find great text and share what they love to read. Not every reader writes long blog posts about their favorite book, but many are inspired to choose a new book because of a compelling Facebook post from a friend or a review on Amazon.com. Reading partnerships evolve over the course of a reader's life, and students should understand all of the ways to find like-minded readers who can share in their love of a text.

Social media can be used in all classrooms to facilitate reading partnerships. Establishing online spaces gives students a place to respond to reading and post questions for peers who are exploring the same text. If a small group of third grade students is reading *Because of Winn-Dixie* in a literature circle, they can practice social media skills by discussing the book through online forums such as Edmodo, Schoology, or Google Classroom.

Although students might interact with text in different languages, love for reading and storytelling is a common thread across cultures. From video conferencing to text messaging, readers can connect in a way previous generations would have found hard to imagine. Connecting readers from around the world gives students a glimpse of children who may have lives that are very similar to or different from their own.

World Read-Aloud Day

At LitWorld, we're working to foster global partnerships by hosting an event called World Read-Aloud Day. Since 2010, readers of all ages from around the world have participated. Many even share their stories and read aloud experiences with us on social media. Log onto litworld.org for more information.

Activity: Global Read Aloud

Goals:

- Students will listen to you model a new skill and develop a passion for reading.
- Students will develop a global reading community without leaving the classroom.

Preparation:

- To find a partner classroom, connect with a former classmate, find a fellow elementary school teacher on Twitter, or send an email to the contact page of an international school in another country.
- Choose a book that explores a shared topic of interest. Perhaps it has a theme that is relatable to both cultures or one that will prompt students to ask a lot of questions.
- Decide how you will connect your class. There is a variety of free video conferencing software to choose from including Skype™, Hangouts™, or FaceTime®.
- Discuss with the other classroom teacher how you will lead the read aloud. Maybe you will split the reading of the book or you will take turns over the course of the school year.

Steps for Success:

1. Connect the classrooms using a predetermined video conferencing platform.

2. While reading, or after the book is finished, ask students from each class to share their responses to a prompt about the book. Depending on the grade level of your students and the book you've chosen, you may want to preread the book with your class and have them prepare responses to share with the other class.

Remember: When video conferencing with students, make sure that you have permission from caregivers for students to participate.

Speaking and Listening

It turns out that talk isn't so cheap! Any time students are using language, whether speaking or listening, they are increasing their capacity for reading and writing. Speaking and listening skills are integral parts of becoming college and career ready; just as students will be required to sift through large amounts of written information, they will also have to interact with many different types of people, in many different environments, with many types of distractions, and still be able to extract the heart of what is being communicated. Decades of research confirms that children can understand and talk about complex ideas conveyed to them orally before they can understand the same ideas expressed on the page. Even more significantly, Sticht and James (1984) found that this gap persists "well into middle school" (Fisher and Frey 2014), which means that the responsibility of effective oral-language development does not lie solely with early education teachers. Speaking and listening must be incorporated into every aspect of the reading curriculum at every grade level.

The potential payoff of this shift in emphasis is supported by research by Wolf, Crossen, and Resnick (2004), which shows that scaffolded classroom talk "assists students to deepen their understanding of texts" and "allows for a rigorous lesson" (Mills 2009). The researchers also reference empirical evidence that dialogic instruction, in which teachers use authentic and open-ended questions paired with academically challenging tasks, are "positively related to develop students' literacy skills" (Applebee et al. 2003). For example, rather than ask a question like *What are two things the mother never does?* when discussing Jean Little's poem "About Loving," a teacher could ask *Why isn't love simple?* This question sparks a conversation in which students can build upon the thoughts and opinions expressed by their peers instead of nodding passively as one student provides the objectively correct response. Frey and Fisher recommend that "about 50 percent of the instructional minutes devoted to content area learning be used for collaborative conversation with peers" (2014).

Social readers are able to talk about what they've read and provide evidence to support their thinking. This is the stepping stone to writing about reading. Talking about reading can provide a much needed foundation for students who are conversationally proficient in the English language, but may struggle to express their ideas as easily as some. The speaking opportunities teachers provide to students can vary greatly. Students might think-pair-share before contributing to a class discussion or have teacher-facilitated small-group conversations to talk about what they've read with just a few of their peers.

When students are interested in their reading materials, they will have more to say on the subject. Teachers can pair high-interest topics for reading materials with video explorations. Leveraging students' sense of curiosity around a topic will create an environment where discussions bring out the voices of all students.

Strengthening Listening Skills with Podcasts

Podcasts are audio recordings similar to a radio program and can be used to help students strengthen their listening skills. A wide range of organizations and individuals host podcasts in order to share their thinking around a topic. Teachers can access podcasts through iTunes® and the Podcast app on iOS devices, or through web-based tools. Most individual podcasts have their own site where episodes can stream directly from their webpage.

EdTech Spotlight

Kid-Friendly Podcasts for Classrooms and Families

If you're looking to set up listening stations in your classroom or simply want to share a list of favorites with families, here are a few podcasts worth checking out.

- **Storynory:** This podcast features a new read-aloud story each week, with an archive of dozens to explore. You'll find classics like *Cinderella* and *Snow White* in their list of most recent recordings.

- **Sparkle Stories:** The Sparkle Stories podcast features original stories that are shared weekly.

- **Brains On!:** This science podcast features episodes that address questions your students may have and ideas to make them wonder about the world around them. You'll find episodes featuring titles like "How do you catch a cold?"

- **Stories Podcast:** From Halloween tales to *Jack and the Beanstalk*, the Stories Podcast shares familiar and new tales with kids. It's a great choice for introducing students to classic stories like *Hansel and Gretel*.

- **The Story Home:** This podcast includes episodes that bring tales of all types come to life. Titles include "Sunshine Stories" and "The Seven Ravens."

There are a wide variety of podcasts to choose from. When teaching a specific subject area such as American history or ocean ecosystems, teachers can search for a related podcast to find a clip to share with students. The search feature in iTunes identifies podcast episodes that focus on specific topics.

By listening to a narrator tell a story or an expert discuss a topic, podcasts can help students strengthen their ability to gather information through multimedia.

- **Listening in partners** gives students another person to share a story with. Just as students may sit and read side by side, children can listen to an audio podcast in pairs to gather information or experience a new story.

- **Talking about topics** helps students set a purpose for listening. In the same way students share their thinking about a text, they can respond to the information or story presented in a podcast.

- **Teaching students to replay** is a strategy similar to rereading. Students are using a wide range of media to learn new information. It's important to help students understand how pressing *rewind* can boost their comprehension.

- **Using podcasts at home** is a great way to extend a learning activity. Pick a few kid-friendly podcasts or episodes that can be shared with families to help connect learning in the classroom to activities at home.

Podcasts for Exploring Informational Text

These podcasts cover topics that may be relevant to your work with students. In the same way you would read an article before handing it out to students, you'll want to listen to a clip before playing it for the class.

- TED Radio Hour
- Why I Write
- Stuff You Missed in History Class

Activity: Learning from Podcasts

Goals:

- Students will practice listening skills while learning new information from a podcast.

Preparation:

- Identify a podcast clip that connects with a current classroom topic.

Steps for Success:

1. Introduce students to the idea of podcasts as a way to gather information. You may decide to make connections to your own learning life and share examples of podcasts you listen to.

2. With students, compile a list of things that strong listeners do. This list may include: finding a comfortable spot to sit, doodling or drawing pictures, and being respectful of other listeners.

3. Choose a podcast clip to play for your class and set a purpose for listening by saying something like, "We are listening to this podcast to learn more about bioluminescence, a topic we explored when reading about marine ecosystems," or, "Let's listen to an interview with one of our favorite authors to learn a bit more about her life."

4. For this activity, you may have a set of discussion questions or response prompts prepared for students to work on with a partner. This will provide accountability for the task and a place for students to record their thinking before having a whole class discussion.

Celebrate!

Building a joyous community of readers starts with allowing all students to feel heard and celebrated. To celebrate someone's accomplishment is to provide him or her with courage and motivation to continue. Celebrate accomplishments both large (e.g., the culmination of a reading project) and small. (e.g., "I appreciate how you took turns reading with your partner today.") Teachers may decide to celebrate accomplishments surrounding the following:

- **Stamina:** "We read for more minutes this week."
- **Volume:** "We read many words this week."
- **Engagement:** "We were focused on our reading this week."
- **Comprehension:** "We had great book talks this week."
- **Identity:** "We changed and grew as readers this week."
- **Collaboration:** "We worked well with our partners this week."

Extend the social-emotional support system by encouraging parents and caregivers to host reading celebrations at home, complete with a favorite snack. Help the children associate a reading community with a culture of affirmation and kindness where friendships deepen and an atmosphere of enjoyment and pleasure reigns supreme.

Dear Families,   _____

Let's make reading social and celebratory for all of our children! Whether they are enjoying books independently or sitting next to you while you read a favorite book aloud, children will feel the excitement of reading to share their thoughts and new knowledge with a community of readers.

To be a social reader means that you share your reading life. Encourage your children to share what they are reading with other family members. Encourage them to make a picture of their reading experience and hang it on the fridge. Talk to your kids about how they would like to celebrate their reading. Some questions you can ask are:

- Where do you want to share your reading?

- With whom would you like to share your reading?

- What are you hoping to learn about in this book?

- What kind of celebration can we have for your reading?

Thank you for joining us in the journey to the Five Habits. Use the Five Habits with your children each and every day to help them grow to become lifelong readers!

With appreciation,

Dear Families,   _____

¡Hagamos de la lectura algo social y de celebración para todos nuestros hijos! Ya sea si disfrutan leer libros por sí solos o sentados a su lado mientras usted lee su libro favorito, los niños sentirán la emoción de leer para compartir sus ideas y nuevos conocimientos con una comunidad de lectores.

Ser un lector social significa compartir sus experiencias en la lectura. Anime a sus hijos a que le cuenten a otros miembros de la familia lo que están leyendo. Anímelos a que dibujen sus experiencias en la lectura y póngalos en el refrigerador. Háblenles sobre cómo les gustaría celebrar la lectura. Algunas preguntas que pueden hacer son:

- ¿Dónde quieren celebrar su lectura?

- ¿Con quién te gustaría compartir tu lectura?

- ¿Qué esperas aprender de este libro?

- ¿Cómo te gustaría celebrar tu lectura?

Gracias por acompañarnos en el viaje hacia los Cinco hábitos [Five Habits]. Use con su hijo los Cinco hábitos para ayudarles a crecer y convertirse en un lector asiduo.

Con agradecimiento,

Assessment in the New Era

As the great literacy researcher Donald Graves (1994) once said, "The teacher is the chief learner in the classroom." This chapter will speak to two types of assessments that help teachers learn more about their instruction and its effect on students: formative and performance-based. Digital tools can help formatively assess students, as can the Five Habits rubrics. These rubrics can be used to confer with students, share ongoing updates with parents, debrief with administrators, or plan for small-group instruction. Throughout this book, one theme has remained: It is a blended world, and therefore the world of students' reading should be blended as well. The same holds true for how students are assessed. Teachers must know their students more deeply than ever before and feel confident in assisting them as they tame the wild text.

The following questions can be used as helpful guides while examining the kinds of data that will bring the most fruitful outcomes for each student:

1. **What does the data say?** Unpacking this seemingly simple question begins by organizing data. Some of it will come from the use of the Five Habits rubrics, and some will come from observational notes or other formative tools that include running records and leveling systems. Online tools like the ones described later in this chapter can help organize this data. Are there patterns in student performance across a week or a month? How do the results compare to other students in the class? To the grade level? To the student's previous performance? Is the student where he or she should be for this time of year?

2. **What does the data mean?** Faculty meetings can be used to analyze information with colleagues and present on individual students as case studies. What kinds of next steps will be needed? Which skills are firmly in place, and what continues to be a struggle? When this analysis is done as part of one's regular instructional practice, it will

provide a great deal of specific information to discuss with parents, administrators, and students.

3. **What actions does the data suggest teachers do?** Now that teachers have gone through the steps of determining and analyzing the information, it's time to use this information to inform curricular decisions. Can a difficult concept be retaught in a one-on-one conference? Can a small group of students experiencing challenges work together to practice one of the Five Habits, or is the difficulty extensive enough that the concept should be reintroduced as part of a whole-group lesson? Are there materials and supplies needed in the classroom that would help students grow as readers? By being responsive to data, curriculum can be brought to them rather than simply teaching lesson by lesson in lockstep.

4. **What actions does the data suggest students do?** Providing timely feedback supports the mentor-apprentice relationship, which is vital to a healthy classroom environment. Dignify students by discussing specific steps they can take to build reading capacity across the Five Habits, and invite them into the process of choosing the best route toward improvement. Giving students the opportunity to take ownership of their learning will increase chances of seeing positive results from your formative assessments.

Formative Assessments

In the reading classroom, there are many ways to leverage the power of technology to make sure students understand the teaching objective. The Five Habits rubrics can help teachers identify the skills to look for in their readers and decide what strategies need to be modeled to get students to the next level. For example, on one day, a teacher may have students review text on a tablet and in a print book to make sure they are reading widely. This type of formative assessment can help teachers pinpoint which students need additional support mastering the Five Habits.

When students respond to questions or prompts on a computer or a tablet, teachers can see their answers in real time and determine who needs extra help. In the past, checklists or sticky notes were often used when conferring with students. These are still great ways to check for understanding, but technology can energize and elevate those practices for formative assessment.

Checking for understanding can happen at different times over the school day. Here are three examples of ways to use technology tools to strengthen formative assessment routines.

- **Before a lesson**—use a survey tool like Kahoot! to see what topics students are most interested in learning about. This can help teachers choose read aloud topics that align with students' passions.

- **During a lesson**—use a backchannel tool like TodaysMeet to give students a space to post facts they have learned about a new topic. Reviewing this online space during a lesson will help teachers identify and immediately assist students who need support in developing questions.

- **After a lesson**—use a digital exit slip tool like Socrative to collect responses related to the teaching objectives. Digital exit slips will help teachers understand which students met the goals for the day and who will need additional support.

Tools for Assessing Understanding

- **Swivl™ Recap**: Students respond to prompts using their webcam to capture video.
- **Seesaw**: Students submit their work, including pictures, audio recordings, and text.
- **Google Classroom**: Students complete assignments and respond to prompts.
- **Padlet**: Students post responses to prompts in a collaborative space.

Performance-Based Assessments

Performance-based assessments (PBA) are projects that represent a student's rich reading life through the unique demonstration of understanding. In their reading lives, students will regularly encounter texts that are not made up of words alone. They must consider visual images, text, and music that work together to create a powerful message. The PBA is an exciting way to engage students with their own assessments: demonstrating, showing, modeling, performing, and interacting with the knowledge they are building in a way that helps them understand how they are growing as readers.

Teachers can set the stage for the performance-based assessment by showing the class examples of advertisements that express a clear opinion about a good or a service and include at least one piece of evidence that supports the opinion. For example, the iconic Taylor Swift Got Milk?® advertisement can be used because it has a strong image, expresses a clear opinion about a product, and has a manageable amount of text that works to support the opinion. Once this or another advertisement with a similarly strong image has been chosen, modeling could unfold as follows:

- Read aloud the text accompanying the ad and study the image together to determine the topic.

- Examine the images and words a second time to think about the opinion being expressed about the topic. (e.g., "Even Taylor Swift needs to build her strength by making healthy food choices!")

- Look closely at the images and text for a third time to determine the information that supports the opinion being expressed. In total, teachers and students will have studied the images and words in the ad three separate times, each with a different purpose in mind.

- Finally, students can work independently or in small groups to record their thinking about another advertisement chosen from the teacher's collection. Their responses should include the opinions being expressed in the advertisement and the information presented to support those opinions.

Digital Portfolios

A digital portfolio provides a platform for collecting student work over the course of the school year and makes it easy to share with an audience. Digital portfolios are particulary useful for students in middle school who are getting ready for high school and need a place to show off their accomplishments. Younger students can benefit from digital portfolios as well. Creating a digital portfolio allows students to handpick their strongest pieces from the school year. This gives them a chance to reflect on their work and set goals for the future.

Tools for Creating Digital Projects

- **Spark Video**: Students can make movies that combine their voice with images, icons, and video clips.
- **Book Creator**: Students can create eBooks to publish and share.
- **Explain Everything™**: Students can create tutorials to inform an audience.

The Five Habits Rubrics

The Five Habits Rubrics can help teachers collect authentic data to assist in planning instruction that will move students forward as readers. The rubrics should be shared with students so they are fully enrolled in the process of building their Five Habits. They can also be clipped onto a clipboard or pulled up on a tablet for use while conferring with individual students.

	Emerging	Approaching	Achieving	Exceeding
Reading Widely	• listens to a wide variety of read alouds • browses narrative and nonfiction text • browses digital and traditional text • browses texts that explore other cultures	• chooses to read a text from an unfamiliar subgenre • occasionally reads nonfiction • reads digital and traditional text, though not in a balanced manner • occasionally reads texts that explore other cultures	• consistently reads texts from more than one subgenre • consistently reads nonfiction • balances interactions with digital and print text • consistently reads texts that explore other cultures	• actively seeks out and enjoys text from a variety of subgenres • reads equal parts fiction and nonfiction • is deliberate in engaging both digital and traditional text • reads texts that explore a wide range of other cultures

	Emerging	Approaching	Achieving	Exceeding
Reading Critically	• provides simple statements regarding feelings about a book or reading experience • can identify an author's bias in nonfiction text with support from the teacher	• notices complexity in a text and makes an effort to "read between the lines" • independently identifies an author's bias in nonfiction text	• notices and tracks patterns related to the complexities and layers of a text • independently identifies an author's bias in nonfiction text and provides evidence to support thinking	• creates and revises theories about the complexities and layers (style and purpose of author) of a text • identifies an author's bias in nonfiction text, provides evidence to support thinking, and offers a different perspective on the topic

51696 —Taming the Wild Text

	Emerging	Approaching	Achieving	Exceeding
Reading Deeply	• rereads to improve understanding when prompted • asks questions about the text when prompted • wants to talk about the text • sometimes works to improve reading stamina • describes cross-curricular connections with teacher support • begins to express interest in authors and genres	• occasionally rereads to improve understanding • independently asks questions about the text • talks about the text in reading partnerships or in one-on-one conferences • works to improve reading stamina on a daily basis • identifies cross-curricular connections with teacher support • occasionally expresses interest in authors or genres	• consistently rereads to improve understanding • asks questions about the text and generally seeks out answers • talks meaningfully about the text in book clubs or in class discussions • reads with stamina and focus for a length of time appropriate for grade level • independently identifies cross-curricular connections • consistently identifies and describes connections to authors or genres	• returns to familiar texts to find new meaning • independently uses a range of sources to seek answers to questions • engages enthusiastically in discussion about the text • reads with stamina and focus for a length of time that exceeds grade level norms • independently identifies and describes cross-curricular connections • passionately connects with authors and genres

	Emerging	Approaching	Achieving	Exceeding
Reading Closely	• records annotations that are unrelated to content or theme • unable to cite text, or cites incorrect text when finding evidence to support thinking	• occasionally records meaningful annotations • cites large chunks of written text to support thinking	• consistently records meaningful annotations • cites precise pieces of written text to support thinking	• tracks several threads of analysis with differentiated, meaningful annotations • cites the most relevant textual evidence to support thinking and describes its validity

	Emerging	Approaching	Achieving	Exceeding
Reading Socially	• creates a short term, immediate plan: "I am going to read with Joe now."	• reads with a partner in mind: "I am going to recommend this book to Joe."	• reads with a short-term goal in mind: "I will connect with Joe to talk more about the series we both love."	• reads with a long-term, self-defined connections to others in mind: "When I read I think about how Joe and I can create a book club or longer book talks."

Final Thoughts

Please keep in mind that in this era of learning, assessment can and should feel as natural as any other action in the classroom. There is no need to stop and go, to "prep" students, or to have them feel assessment takes them away from the meaningful work of the day. Assessment should be seen as a valuable tool for mutual learning, filled with the joy and engagement of reading itself, unlocking clues to the success of each reader and leading to success for all.

Next Steps

We have explored the Five Habits for Readers in this new, amazing time of reading instruction. You are now ready to begin. Take this work back to your classroom and use all you have learned to help your students tame the wild text. We leave you with eight action steps for implementation to help you feel fully prepared to set off on your journey of learning with your students.

1. Create a **professional learning community** of colleagues who wish to join you in this exploration. Set aside time to read widely, critically, deeply, closely, and socially with your peers.

2. Formatively **assess students** to identify areas of strength and challenge. When assessing, remember that digital reading checklists can replace clipboards, and digital exit slips can replace sticky notes.

3. Learn how to use **communication platforms** such as Pinterest, Facebook, and Twitter so that you can be well versed in social media skills yourself. Use these platforms to conduct your own professional learning online.

21st Century Communication Platforms

Keep all of your ideas in one place with content curated online. Collect and share boards, ideas, and information with other educators.

Facebook
- Use the Groups tool to further professional development or learn about new topics of interest.
- Stay connected to individuals that have aided in your growth and mindset as an educator.

Twitter
- Search for relevant topics, and follow thought leaders to get ideas about who is sharing great content.
- Use hashtags to locate information grouped on a particular topic and to chat with the education community.
- For the ultimate guide on Twitter in education, take a look at *140 Twitter Tips for Educators* by Brad Currie, Billy Krawokwer, and Scott Rocco.

Favorite Educational Hashtags

#edtech (education techology)
#readaloud (favorite books)
#ADEchat (Apple® products)
#ELLchat (English Language Learners)

4. **Set clear goals** for planning in reading instruction. With your professional learning community, create a timeline of when to introduce each of the Five Habits. Look at your curriculum map for the year, and plan with standards in mind. For example, if you teach a nonfiction unit of study, you may choose to introduce students to the habit of reading critically as you explore persuasive text.

5. **Set dates for reading celebrations.** Invite parents and administrators to share in the students' excitement about their accomplishments. An authentic audience encourages students to read critically, deeply, and closely.

6. Use centralized **collaborative planning documents** so you can establish a strategy plan with colleagues, solicit feedback, and check in on student understanding. Your school may already use a cloud-based system like Box, G Suite from Google Cloud or Dropbox™, but if not, it's easy and free to set up an online space to collect your favorite resources. When you plan collaboratively, you can build off the ideas of your grade-level team and tweak lessons to fit the needs of your group of students.

7. **Advocate** for your students to have access to high-quality literature in all genres on all platforms. Searching for just-right resources is an important part of planning for purposeful reading instruction. Talk with your administrators about how to best allocate funds for classroom reading materials. Research online book collections that offer discounted or free subscriptions for educators.

8. **Choose technology tools** that connect to your learning goals and address the needs of all students. Revisit the callout boxes in each chapter as well as the resources listed in Appendix D to find apps and websites that support your learning goals.

Resources for Accessing Your Standards Online

- MasteryConnect Standards-by-State Apps
- Common Core State Standards

Teacher Takeaways

Refer to Appendix A on pages 133–141 to access documents designed to help teachers examine their practices. This task of reflection and goal setting may be something teachers take on as part of a personal professional-development plan. Alternatively, this work could be brought into professional learning communities within a school or simply explored with a colleague.

Choosing Technology Tools

Technology tools can provide a fantastic set of interventions for students who are working toward mastery. When choosing apps and web tools for students, there a few important things to keep in mind:

- Is this tool age-appropriate? Will older students find it too babyish and turn off to reading?
- Does this tool work students through levels? Is there a baseline quiz to make sure they are following a personalized pathway?
- Can the teacher check on their progress? If students are asked to answer questions, is there a teacher dashboard or a way to see what they've mastered?
- Can this tool be used in different languages? Will switching the language of a tool help or hinder students as readers?
- Is there an audio function that will prompt or support students? Will an audio tool help students or become a crutch for them?

Independent Reading Tips

- Read for social change. Invite students to choose a topic/theme for changing the world, and then see how their reading connects to that.

- Orchestrate and coach partner conversations between students about a text's themes and ideas.

- Celebrate your students' reading accomplishments (with certificates and other types of recognition) and honor milestones for independence, both big and small.

References

AAP Council On Communications and Media. 2016. "Media and Young Minds." *Pediatrics.* 138 (5): doi: 10.1521

Applebee, Arthur N., Judith A. Langer, Martin Nystrand, and Adam Gamoran. 2003. "Discussion-Based Approaches to Developing Understanding: Classroom Instruction and Student Performance in Middle and High School English." *American Educational Research Journal* 40: 685-730.

Bishop, Rudine Sims. 1990. "Mirrors, Windows, and Sliding Glass Doors." *Perspectives: Choosing and Using Books for the Classroom* 6 (3). https://www.psdschools.org/webfm/8559.

Bos, Candace S., and Sharon Vaughn. 2005. *Strategies for Teaching Students with Learning and Behavioral Problems,* 6th ed. Boston: Allyn & Bacon.

Bus, Adriana G., Zsofia K. Takacs, and Cornelia A.T. Kegel. 2015. "Affordances and Limitations of Electronic Storybooks for Young Children's Emergent Literacy." *Developmental Review* 35: 79–97.

Chen, Chih-Ming, and Fang-Ya Chen. 2014. "Enhancing Digital Reading Performance with a Collaborative Reading Annotation System." *Computers & Education* 77: 67–81.

Duke, Nell K. 2003. "Reading to Learn from the Very Beginning: Informational Books in Early Childhood." *Young Children* 58 (2): 14–20.

Engel, Susan. 2015. *The Hungry Mind: The Origins of Curiosity in Childhood.* Cambridge, MA. Harvard University Press.

Frey, Nancy, and Douglas Fisher. 2014. "Speaking and Listening in Content Area Learning," *The Reading Teacher* 68 (1). 64–69

Gaver, William W. 1991. "Technology Affordances." *Proceedings of CHI'91* ACM, New York (New Orleans, Louisiana, April 28–May 2): 79-84. https://www.lri.fr/~mbl/Stanford/CS477/papers/Gaver-CHI1991.

Guernsey, Lisa, and Michael H. Levine. 2015. "Tap, Click, Read: Growing Readers in a World of Screens." San Francisco: Jossey-Bass. Kindle edition.

Hodgson, Kevin. 2010. "Strategies for Online Reading Comprehension." *Learn NC*. http://www.learnnc.org/lp/pages/6958.

Jabr, Ferris. 2013. "The Reading Brain in the Digital Age: The Science of Paper versus Screens," *Scientific American* https://www.scientificamerican.com/article/reading-paper-screens/.

Kellogg, Carolyn. 2015. "6 Book Trends for 2016: Look into the Future." *Los Angeles Times*.

Konnikova, Maria. 2014. "Being a Better Online Reader." *New Yorker.* July 16. http://www.newyorker.com/science/maria-konnikova/being-a-better-online-reader.

Lee, June, and Brigid Barron. 2015. "Aprendiendo en Casa: Media as a Resource for Learning Among Hispanic-Latino Families." *A Report of the Families and Media Project.* New York: The Joan Ganz Cooney Center at Sesame Workshop.

Mills, Kathy A. 2009. "Floating on a Sea of Talk: Reading Comprehension Through Speaking and Listening." *The Reading Teacher* 63. (4): 325–329.

National Education Association. "Using Text Structure." Accessed July 3, 2017, http://www.nea.org/tools/using-text-structure.html.

OECD. 2015. *Students, Computers and Learning: Making the Connection.* Paris. OECD Publishing.

Schugar, Heather Ruetschlin, Carol A. Smith, and Jordan T. Schugar. 2013. "Teaching With Interactive Picture E-Books in Grades K–6." *The Reading Teacher* 66 (8): 615–624.

Simpson, Alyson, Maureen Walsh, and Jennifer Rowsell. 2013. "The Digital Reading Path: Researching Modes and Multidirectionality with iPads." *Literacy* 47 (3): 123-130.

Sticht, T. G., and J. H. James. 1984. "Listening and Reading," *Handbook of Reading Research*, vol. 1, edited by P. David Pearson, Rebecca Barr, Michaela Kamil, and Peter Mosenthal. 293-317.

Toyama, Kentaro. 2015. *Geek Heresy: Rescuing Social Change from the Cult of Technology*. New York: PublicAffairs.

Wolf, Maryanne, and Mirit Barzillai. 2009. "The Importance of Deep Reading," *Educational Leadership* 66 (6): 32–37.

Wolf, Mikyung Kim, Amy C. Crosson, and Lauren B. Resnick. 2004. "Classroom Talk for Rigorous Reading Comprehension Instruction." *Reading Psychology* 26 (1): 27–53.

Wolpert, Gloria, and Lisa Anne Vacca-Rizopoulos. 2012. "Assessing Narrative and Expository Reading Passages by Text and Online Presentation." *American International Journal of Contemporary Research* 2 (4): 39–46.

Teacher Takeaways

Finding a Balance of Text Types

Take stock of your current classroom library or digital bookshelf.

Record the types of text students have access to. Place a P next to print resources and a D next to digital resources.

Fiction	Nonfiction

What items are missing from your classroom library or digital bookshelf?

_____

_____

_____

_____

_____

Introducing New Text Types

Reflect on "new" text types that you have introduced to students.

Record the ways you have already used a text type or the way you plan on using it in the future.

Blog Posts	Tweets
Facebook Posts	**Infographics**
Online News Articles	**eBooks**

Evaluating Sources

Make a plan for how you can think aloud as you evaluate sources with your students.

Record the topic you wish to explore with your students, the sources you will share with them, and the think aloud questions you will model.

Topic: _____

Sources (ex. print/digital newspaper article, print/digital short passage, website)	Think-Aloud Questions *How will you show students the ways a reader evaluates a new text?*
Source A:	**Question #1:** **Question #2:** **Question #3:**
Source B:	**Question #1:** **Question #2:** **Question #3:**
Source C:	**Question #1:** **Question #2:** **Question #3:**

Cross-Curricular Connections

Make a plan for connecting a social studies or a science topic with your reading instruction.

Choose a primary source document, a piece of literature, or informational text that connects to a reading goal.

Text Type (ex. primary source document, piece of literature, or informational text):

Reading Goal (ex. explore point of view, evaluate a source):

How will students interact with this text? (print/digital)

How does this text connect to your learning goals?

Preparing Students to Use Text-Based Evidence

Design a lesson where you will model how to lift a line from a text to support your thinking.

Record the information you will share with students and your plan for the lesson.

Title of Text:
Prompt or Question:
Your response to the prompt or question:
Evidence from the text that supports your answer:
What will you expect students to do when they support their answer with text evidence?
Does your model align with student expectations? If yes, how? If no, what can you add?

Preparing Students for Digital Reading Responses

Make a plan for introducing digital reading responses to students.

Use the table below to organize your thinking before introducing students to the concept of responding to their reading with digital tools.

Instructional Goals (ex. use text evidence, make text-to-text connections):
Prompt or Question:
Digital Tools Students Will Use:
What should students include in their response?
What type of preparation will students have to take in order to complete the response?
How will students share their digital reading response with others?
Have you created an exemplar to share with students?

Virtual Reality Prereading Teacher Brainstorming Sheet

Make a plan for introducing virtual reality to students.

Use the table below to organize your thinking before introducing students to the concept of using virtual reality as a tool for prereading.

What book are you sharing with students?
Describe the setting(s) of the book:
Digital Tools Students Will Use
Name any important places that are referenced in the book:
What type of virtual reality experience could help students better understand the setting or a big idea from this book?

Virtual Reality Content I've Found	**How It Connects to the Text**

What did you choose to share with your class? How will this help them better understand the text?

Passionate Readers Activity

Make a plan for introducing digital reading responses to students.

Use the table below to organize your thinking before introducing students to the concept of responding to their reading with digital tools.

Book Title_____

Interesting Moments In the Book	This Makes Me Wonder...

51696 —Taming the Wild Text

Example Lesson Plans

Reading Widely Lesson

Lesson Objective

Readers compare and contrast the characteristics of two genres of literature.

Lesson Purpose (Authentic and Transferrable)

- Students will identify characteristics of literature.
- Students will distinguish between two genres.

Student Work (Check for understanding)

- Graphic organizer (interactive concept map and/or text-based response)

Teacher Notes

In this lesson, students will compare and contrast two genres of literature. Students will read two examples of text and document their thinking, using a digital graphic organizer. As you examine the best way to integrate technology into your lesson, you may have students use shared screens to complete a concept map together or shared digital text using a QR code posted in a class learning-management system like Google Classroom. The purpose of using technology in this lesson is to give students a customizable space to organize their thinking. Technology tools used in this fashion provide you with opportunities to view learning pathways of your students and provide flexibility for differentiation.

In a K–2 classroom… First, share a read aloud from two genres, such as fantasy and realistic fiction. Then, introduce a digital space where students can add what they notice about the two different readings.

Students then use a voice-recording tool like Drawp to add their thinking to graphic organizers. They tap the screen to add examples from each text to provide evidence of genre. Students can work on individual devices or collaboratively with a partner.

In a 3–5 classroom… First, introduce two short passages from different genres. For example, one could be science fiction and the other could be historical fiction. Have the class discuss the characteristics of each genre and work in pairs to find examples from each passage that support their thinking.

Students can use a screencasting tool like Explain Everything™ to snap a picture of the text and annotate it as they record their voice to document their thinking. Their screencast can conclude with a Venn diagram that compares and contrasts characteristics of the two genres.

In a 6–8 classroom… First, distribute a digital text to students by linking the passages you have located online to a QR code.

Students scan the QR codes to view a personal narrative and a memoir. Students use the Make-a-Map tool in BrainPOP to create a concept map that links common characteristics of each genre and identifies key elements that distinguish one from another. Students can include images to support their thinking in addition to evidence from the text.

Reading Critically Lesson

Lesson Objective

Readers evaluate an author's bias by examining their background and previous work.

Lesson Purpose (Authentic and Transferrable)

- Students will explore author bias.
- Students will read with a critical eye.

Student Work (Check for understanding)

- Interactive reading response (voice recording and/or text-based response)

Teacher Notes

In this lesson, students will evaluate an author's bias as they examine the author's background and previous work. Students will read a text from an author that has an accessible biography and other published work to reflect on how this author's past experience influences her writing.

As you examine the best way to integrate technology into your lesson, you may decide to have students annotate text using digital devices or snap pictures of text to capture their thinking.

The purpose of using technology in this lesson is to give students options for interacting with text and crafting a response. Technology tools used in this fashion provide students with an opportunity to annotate text and capture their thinking.

In a K–2 classroom… First, model how to use the About the Author section of a book to learn about the author's background. Collect several titles written by this author to help students see connections between topics.

Students can use prompts for discussion and reflection, such as "I think this author wrote this book because _____" or "Since I know this fact about the author,_____." Students can write their sentences or record their thoughts using an app like ChatterPix Kids.

In a 3–5 classroom… First, model how to use an author's biography or his or her LinkedIn profile to learn about the author's background. Gather a few articles by this writer to share with students. After student pairs dive into the articles, bring them back together to discuss how the topics or perspectives of the articles connect to what they've learned about the writer's life. Students can compose a series of questions in the form of tweets to learn more about the writer's interests and potential bias.

In a 6–8 classroom… First, model how to use an author's biography or her LinkedIn profile to learn about her background. Gather a few articles by this writer to share with students. After student pairs dive into the articles, bring them back together to discuss how the topics or perspectives of the articles connect to what they've learned about the writer's life. Students can compose a series of questions in the form of tweets to learn more about the writer's interests and potential bias.

Reading Deeply Lesson

Lesson Objective

Readers connect with a historical figure who has impacted them as they trace how this person changes over time.

Lesson Purpose (Authentic and Transferrable)
- Students will make personal connections to a historical figure.
- Students will locate text evidence to support their thinking.

Student Work (Check for understanding)
- Annotated time line (illustrated response and/or text-based response)

Teacher Notes

Students who read deeply have an interest and passion in the subject matter. They feel connected to their reading on a deeper, more meaningful level. In this lesson, students will investigate a historical figure through multiple texts. Give students a choice on whom to investigate as they begin this reading journey. As they read about the way this person changes over time, they will compare their own life experiences to this individual. Students will document their thinking on an annotated time line. As they move across the time line, they will add their own life experiences that mirror that of the historical figure they have chosen.

As you examine the best way to integrate technology into your lesson, you may decide to have students illustrate a time line or combine images to demonstrate how a historical figure changed over time.

The purpose of using technology in this lesson is to give students a way to capture their thinking through multimedia. Technology tools used in this fashion provide students with a range of ways to demonstrate their understanding.

In a K–2 classroom... First, choose a selection about a historical figure who changes throughout the text. Then, model your thinking as you read a nonfiction selection about this person. While reading, draw a time line to document the key events in the person's life. As you think aloud, point out evidence of when the historical figure changes over the course of the text. Discuss how this reminds you of moments in your own life.

As students dive into their own reading, provide them with options of historical figures who have life stories similar to theirs. Students can use an illustration or a poster-making tool on their devices to combine drawings, images, and text to create a collage-like representation of how a person changed over time.

In a 3–5 classroom... First, choose a selection about a historical figure who changes throughout the text. As you read aloud and model your thinking, jot down key moments that reflect how the person changes. Add a note about how it connects to your life.

Provide student pairs with books about historical figures who have similar life stories to theirs. As students read, they can search for images and icons that represent moments when the person changed. They can use a moviemaking tool like Spark Video to combine images, icons, and text. The narration feature in this tool lets students record their voices to elaborate on the images and icons they chose. Ask students to use the last 20 seconds of their video to state a final personal connection to the historical figure and questions for further investigation.

In a 6–8 classroom... First, use a short text to model your thinking about how a historical figure has changed as a result of the events in the passage. Pause to think aloud about connections to your own life. Provide students with texts about historical figures with whom students may be able to make a connection.

Students can use collaborative Google Docs in small groups to brainstorm events from the text that relate to how this person changes. They can add in connections to their own life experiences in different colors to compare and contrast the ways they are connected. In this small group, students can locate evidence from the text to support their thinking and use this information to create a Google Slides presentation. Encourage students to use images and color to convey the mood of the text. Ask students to include a final slide with questions they would ask this person if they had the chance.

Reading Closely Lesson

Lesson Objective

Readers identify character traits using evidence to support their thinking.

Lesson Purpose (Authentic and Transferrable)

- Students will identify traits that describe a character.
- Students will use text evidence to support their thinking.

Student Work (Check for understanding)

- Digital exit slip (video reflection and/or text-based response)

Teacher Notes

In this lesson, students will identify important character traits, using evidence to support their thinking. Students will read a print text and document their thinking using a variety of modalities that include the camera, a drawing, or a typed response.

As you examine the best way to integrate technology into your lesson you may have students explore digital texts instead of traditional print books. Additionally, if you only have access to a few tablets, you may have students respond to reading as part of station rotation.

The purpose of using technology in this lesson is to capture student thinking in an authentic manner. Technology tools used in this fashion provide teachers with opportunities to differentiate their instruction by giving options for audio, video, and text-based responses to reading.

In a K–2 classroom… First, model close reading with a picture book read aloud, showing students how you pay close attention to the character. Using a video reflection tool like Seesaw, model how to record yourself using the camera on your tablet.

Students then read their own picture books independently or with a partner. As their reading comes to a close, have them open the Seesaw app and record a video reflection where they talk about their main character and a character trait they identified, pointing to the page in the book to show their text evidence.

In a 3–5 classroom… First, open an excerpt from a chapter book on an interactive whiteboard, and model your thinking as you name a character trait and highlight evidence in the text to support your thinking. Write a few sentences to capture your thinking, and remind students of the procedure for sending a digital exit slip.

Students then sit with their literature circles to discuss characters in their own books, swiping through the virtual pages as they discuss. At the end of their discussion, students highlight a passage that provides evidence of a character trait and compose digital exit slips to share their thinking with you.

In a 6–8 classroom… First, share a short story with students through Google Classroom so that each student can open up a copy on his or her device. Model your thinking as you examine the main character and identify a character trait. Use text evidence to support your thinking.

Students then discuss the second half of the passage in pairs before turning to their own device to highlight text evidence and leave a comment with their thinking. You are able to review the comments on the shared document to monitor student responses.

Reading Socially Lesson

Lesson Objective

Readers notice and use informational text features to conduct research on a topic as they work to create a public service announcement.

Lesson Purpose (Authentic and Transferrable)

- Students will identify informational text features.
- Students will gather information for persuasive writing.

Student Work (Check for understanding)

- Public service announcement (video clip)

Teacher Notes

In this lesson, students will use informational text features to conduct research on a topic as they prepare to create a public service announcement. Students will explore digital and print examples of informational text as they read to learn about a topic.

As you examine the best way to integrate technology into your lesson, you may decide to have students interact with either digital or print text or a combination of both types.

The purpose of using technology in this lesson is to give students a way to interact with a variety of text features and create a final product that sets a purpose for their reading. Technology tools used in this fashion provide students with different ways to interact with text and create a product.

In a K–2 classroom… First, model how to identify text features like the table of contents and captions. Use a document camera to show print examples to the whole class or model your thinking as you explore a digital text on an interactive whiteboard.

Students can use sticky notes in print books or the highlighting tool in digital text to mark up places in their text that provide interesting information on the topic. Students can share the information they learned as they record a 15-second video. Combine each student's contribution to create a class video.

In a 3–5 classroom… After a previous exploration of informational text features in print books, introduce students to digital text features. Model how to use digital text features, like hyperlinks and interactive diagrams, to locate additional information on a topic.

As students prepare to create public service announcements, they can organize their research and ideas using a tool like Popplet. Students can color-code their argument and sequence their thinking as they develop a script and prepare to record their videos.

In a 6–8 classroom… First, model how you navigate information posted on the Internet. Think aloud as you explore content linked from a home page to external resources, and use text features to evaluate the strength of the resource.

Have students search the Internet for specific information that can be used in their public service announcement. This information can be organized on a cloud-based note-taking tool like Evernote. As students review the information they've collected, they can create a plan for their public service announcement using a tool like Storyboard That.

Student Reproducible Sheets

Interest Survey 6-8

How would you describe yourself as a reader?

_____

_____

When you visit a library, what sections do you go to most often?

_____

_____

Do you prefer to read paperback books or e-books on a tablet/smartphone?

_____

_____

If you've read a new book or an interesting article online, whom do you usually talk to about what you've read?

_____

_____

_____

_____

Do you have a favorite author, genre, or topic you like to read about?

_____

_____

_____

Interest Survey 3–5

What types of books do you like to read?

_____

_____

What is one of your favorite books? Why do you love this book?

_____

_____

Do you like reading books with stories or books full of facts?

_____

_____

What genres do you like to read?

_____

_____

What topics do you like to learn about?

_____

_____

Interest Survey K-2

Directions: Circle your answers.

I like books that are:

Funny   Scary   Exciting

I like books with:

People   Animals   Magic

Draw your answer:

I like reading to learn about...

Reading a Blog Post

Blog: _____

Author: _____

What have we learned about the topic? _____

_____

_____

_____

Who is the author, and why did he or she write this post? _____

_____

_____

_____

Where else can I go to get more information on this topic? _____

_____

_____

_____

Infographic

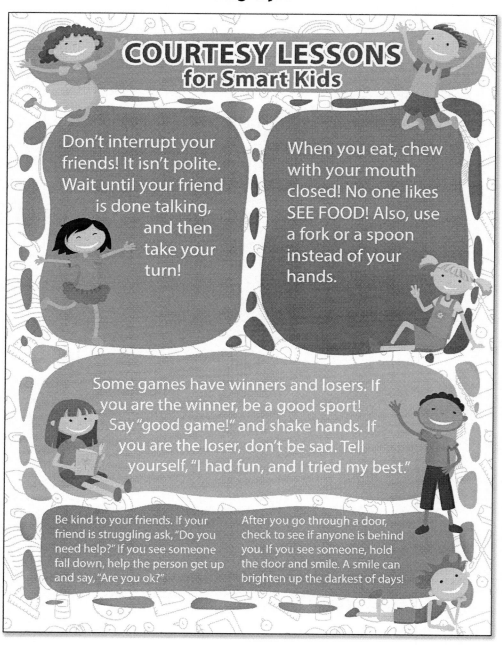

COURTESY LESSONS for Smart Kids

Don't interrupt your friends! It isn't polite. Wait until your friend is done talking, and then take your turn!

When you eat, chew with your mouth closed! No one likes SEE FOOD! Also, use a fork or a spoon instead of your hands.

Some games have winners and losers. If you are the winner, be a good sport! Say "good game!" and shake hands. If you are the loser, don't be sad. Tell yourself, "I had fun, and I tried my best."

Be kind to your friends. If your friend is struggling ask, "Do you need help?" If you see someone fall down, help the person get up and say, "Are you ok?"

After you go through a door, check to see if anyone is behind you. If you see someone, hold the door and smile. A smile can brighten up the darkest of days!

Reading an Infographic

Infographic Title: _____

Creator: _____

Where was it found? _____

What is the big idea of this infographic?

_____

_____

What does the creator of this infographic want me to know?

_____

_____

Why might an author include this infographic in his or her article?

_____

_____

_____

How else could the creator of this infographic represent this information?

_____

_____

_____

Creating an Infographic

Topic: _____

Survey questions:

_____

_____

_____

Survey results:

_____

_____

_____

What big message would you like your infographic to get across?

_____

_____

What type of icons or images could you use?

_____

_____

What type of colors or fonts could you use?

_____

_____

Name _____ Date _____

Genre Bingo

Choose a book that you are interested in reading. After completing it, determine which genre it is. Then, fill in the correct bingo card square with the title and author. Your goal is to do any or all of these:

- read all the genres in one column
- read all the genres in one row
- read all the genres in a diagonal row
- blackout: read ALL the genres on the Bingo card

BINGO

HISTORICAL FICTION	NONFICTION	FANTASY	SPORTS FICTION
MYSTERY	POETRY	NARRATIVE	BIOGRAPHY
HOW-TO	FICTION	FOLK TALE	FICTION IN A SERIES
SCIENCE FICTION	FANTASY	PERSUASIVE	REALISTIC FICTION

Primary Source Analysis

Title of document: _____

When is it from? _____

What do I know about this time period? _____

_____

_____

_____

_____

What do I notice? _____

_____

_____

_____

_____

What do I wonder? _____

_____

_____

_____

_____

Keyword Search

Topic: _____

Question	Keywords to help me find my answer

Fact Finding Reflection

1. Fact: _____

_____

Website Citation: _____

2. Fact: _____

_____

Website Citation: _____

3. Fact: _____

_____

Website Citation: _____

Virtual Reality Prereading

Website Citation: _____

Before Your Field Trip:

Where are you going on your virtual reality field trip?

_____

What do you already know about this place or topic?

_____

_____

After Your Field Trip:

What did you see?

_____

_____

_____

_____

What do you wonder about this place or topic?

_____

_____

_____

_____

If you could have used other senses like touch, smell, or taste, how would this experience be different?

_____

_____

Virtual Reality Prereading
Teacher Brainstorming Sheet

What book are you sharing with students? _____

Describe the setting(s) of the book: _____
_____

Name any important places that are referenced in the book: _____
_____

What type of virtual reality experience could help students better understand the
setting or a big idea from this book? _____
_____
_____

Virtual Reality Content I've Found	How It Connects to the Text

Put a star next to the content you've chosen to share with your class. How will
this help them better understand the text? _____
_____
_____
_____

Read Aloud Planning Page

What text are you reading? _____

When in text will you pause?	What questions will you ask during your think aloud?

What will your follow-up look like? _____

_____

_____

_____

_____

Close Reading for Multiple Perspectives

Book Title: _____

Character: _____

Situation: _____

_____

_____

What would your character say in this situation?

_____

_____

_____

Why would your character say this?

_____

_____

_____

What in the text supports your thinking? Include page or paragraph numbers.

_____

_____

_____

_____

Digital Anchor Charts

What did you find in our resource library today?

_____

_____

How can these resources help you as a learner?

_____

_____

What do you wish were in our digital resource library?

_____

_____

How easy is it to find what you're looking for?

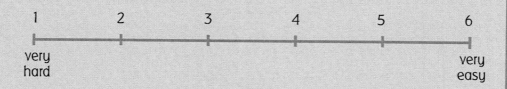

| 1 | 2 | 3 | 4 | 5 | 6 |

very
hard

very
easy

Book Trailer Brainstorming Sheet

Title: _____

Author: _____

What is this book about? _____

_____

_____

What type of reader might enjoy this book? _____

_____

What should someone know about this book? _____

_____

_____

Three words that describe this book:

_____, _____, and _____.

What is the mood of this book?

_____

_____

_____

Book Trailer Storyboard Template

Title: _____

Author: _____

What will I put on my slide? (text, icons, images, illustrations)

_____

_____

_____

_____

What will I say? (script for narration) _____

_____

_____

_____

_____

_____

_____

_____

_____

_____

_____

Hashtag Reading Response

Book Title: _____

Author: _____

Response to teacher or choice prompt:

_____

_____

_____

_____

_____

_____

Brainstorm hashtags:

•

•

•

Why did you choose to include these hashtags on your response?

_____

_____

_____

Tweeting the Read Aloud

Book Title: _____

Author: _____

Response to Prompt:

_____

_____

_____

_____

_____

_____

_____

_____

_____

_____

Concise Response (140 characters or less):

_____

_____

_____

Learning from Podcasts

Name of Podcast: _____

Episode Title: _____

What was the big idea behind this episode?

_____

_____

What did you learn about the topic?

_____

_____

_____

_____

How does the information presented in the podcast connect to our classwork?

_____

_____

_____

What new questions do you have?

_____

_____

_____

Resources and Tech Tools

Features of this Book

- **LitWorld:** www.litworld.org

Chapter 1: Reading Widely

Digital Options for Interest Surveys
- **Google Form:** https://www.google.com/forms/about/
- **Socrative:** https://www.socrative.com/
- **Kahoot:** https://getkahoot.com/

Resources for Kid-Friendly Feature Articles
- **Newsela:** https://newsela.com/
- **News-O-Matic:** https://newsomatic.org/
- **Smithsonian Tween Tribune:** http://tweentribune.com/
- **TIME for Kids:** http://www.timeforkids.com/

Tools for Locating Infographics
- **Kids Discover:** http://www.kidsdiscover.com/
- *Infographics: Human Body* by Peter Grundy https://www.amazon.com /Infographics-Human-Body-Peter-Grundy/dp/1848776551
- **Reading Rocket's Infographic Board:** http://www.readingrockets.org/

Tools for Creating Infographics
- **Keynote:** http://www.apple.com/keynote/
- **Canva:** https://www.canva.com/
- **Pages:** http://www.apple.com/pages/

Resources for Reading at Home
- **Newsela:** https://newsela.com/
- **YouTube** (search "read alouds")**:** https://www.youtube.com /results?search_query=read+alouds
- **StorylineOnline:** http://www.storylineonline.net/
- **OceanHouse Media:** http://www.oceanhousemedia.com/
- **News-O-Matic:** https://newsomatic.org/
- **iBooks Children's Category:** https://itunes.apple.com/us/genre/books-kids /id11086?mt=11

Subscription-Based Digital Libraries
- **EPIC!:** https://www.getepic.com/
- **News-O-Matic:** https://newsomatic.org/
- **Reading Rainbow:** https://www.readingrainbow.com/
- **DK Readers:** https://www.dk.com/us/
- **Explor-eBook:** http://www.teachercreatedmaterials.com/administrators /myesplor-ebook/

Resources for Early Digital Readers
- **Website:** Joan Ganz Cooney Center http://www.joanganzcooneycenter.org/
- **Book:** *Tap, Click, Read* by Lisa Guernsey and Michael H. Levine
      http://www.tapclickread.org/
- **Article:** "Screen Time" by Lisa Guernsey http://www.lisaguernsey.com/screen-time.htm

Research
- **SAMR Model:** https://www.commonsensemedia.org/videos
  /introduction-to-the-samr-model
- **"Aprendiendo en Casa:"** http://www.joanganzcooneycenter.org/wp-content
  /uploads/2015/02/jgcc_aprendiendoencasa.pdf

Chapter 2—Reading Critically

Locating Primary-Source Documents
- **Library of Congress:** https://www.loc.gov/
- **National Archives:** https://www.archives.gov/
- **LIFE Photo Archive:** http://images.google.com/hosted/life

Digital Tools for Notetaking
- **Google Docs:** https://www.google.com/docs/about/
- **Evernote:** https://evernote.com
- **Notability:** http://gingerlabs.com
- **Simplenote:** https://simplenote.com

Voice-to-Text Apps
- **Dragon Dictation:** http://www.dragonmobileapps.com
- **Speechnotes:** https://speechnotes.co
- **Evernote:** https://evernote.com

Digital Tools to Organize Thinking
- **Popplet:** http://popplet.com/
- **BrainPOP Make-a-Map:** https://educators.brainpop.com/video
  /exploring-make-map-concept-mapping-overview-video/
- **Padlet:** https://padlet.com/

Tools with Easy and Automatic Citations
- **Spark Page:** https://spark.adobe.com/
- **Shadow Puppet Edu:** https://itunes.apple.com/us/app/shadow-puppet-edu
  /id888504640?mt=8
- **Haiku Deck:** https://www.haikudeck.com/

Chapter 3—Reading Deeply

Reading Response Apps and Websites
- **ChatterPix Kids:** http://www.duckduckmoose.com/educational-iphone-itouch-apps-for-kids/chatterpixkids/
- **Explain Everything:** https://explaineverything.com/
- **Spark Video:** https://spark.adobe.com/about/video
- **PicCollage:** https://pic-collage.com/
- **Storyboard That:** http://www.storyboardthat.com/
- **Tellagami:** https://tellagami.com/
- **Shadow Puppet Edu:** https://itunes.apple.com/us/app/shadow-puppet-edu/id888504640?mt=8
- **Canva:** https://www.canva.com/
- **SparkPage:** https://spark.adobe.com/

Augmented Reality Apps
- **Quiver:** http://www.quivervision.com
- **Star Walk Kids:** http://vitotechnology.com/star-walk-kids.html
- **Anatomy 4D:** http://anatomy4d.daqri.com
- **Crayola Color Alive:** http://www.crayola.com/splash/products/ColorAlive

Apps to Use with Google Cardboard
- **YouVisit:** http://www.youvisit.com/
- **Nearpod:** https://nearpod.com/
- **Thinglink:** https://www.thinglink.com/
- **NYT VR** https://play.google.com/store/apps/details?id=com.im360nytvr&hl=en
- **Discovery VR**: http://www.discoveryvr.com/

Chapter 4—Reading Closely

Annotation Tools for Students
- **Kami:** https://web.kamihq.com/web/viewer.html
- **iAnnotate:** https://www.iannotate.com/
- **iTunes U:** http://www.apple.com/education/itunes-u/
- **Nearpod:** https://nearpod.com/

Interactive Mapping Tools
- **Popplet:** http://popplet.com/
- **Inspiration Maps:** http://www.inspiration.com/go/ipad
- **BrainPOP Make-a-Map:** https://www.brainpop.com/

Tools for Creating Digital Anchor Charts
- **Spark Post:** https://spark.adobe.com/about/post
- **Canva:** https://www.canva.com/
- **Keynote:** https://www.apple.com/keynote/

Chapter 5—Reading Socially

Tools for Creating a Book Trailer
- **Spark Video:** https://spark.adobe.com/about/video
- **iMovie:** https://www.apple.com/imovie/
- **Shadow Puppet Edu:** http://get-puppet.co

Kid-Friendly Podcasts for Classrooms and Families
- **Storynory:** http://www.storynory.com/
- **Sparkle Stories:** https://www.sparklestories.com/
- **Brains On!:** http://www.brainson.org/
- **Stories Podcast:** http://storiespodcast.com/
- **The Story Home:** http://thestoryhome.com/

Podcasts for Exploring Informational Text
- **TED Radio Hour:** http://www.npr.org/programs/ted-radio-hour/?showDate=2017-02-03
- **Why I Write:** http://whyiwrite.us/category/podcasts/
- **Stuff You Missed in History Class:** http://www.missedinhistory.com/

Chapter 6—Assessment in the New Era

Tools for Assessing Understanding
- **Swivl™ Recap:** https://letsrecap.com
- **Seesaw:** https://web.seesaw.me
- **Google Classroom:** https://edu.google.com/products/productivity-tools/classroom/
- **Padlet:** https://padlet.com

Tools for Creating Digital Projects
- **Spark Video:** https://spark.adobe.com/about/video
- **Book Creator:** https://support.bookcreator.com/hc/en-us
- **Explain Everything:** https://explaineverything.com/app/

Chapter 7—Next Steps

21st Century Communication Platforms
- **Facebook:** http://facebook.com/
- **Twitter:** http://twitter.com/

Resources for Accessing Your Standards Online
- **MasteryConnect Standards-by-State Apps:** https://www.masteryconnect.com/goodies.html
- **Common Core State Standards:** http://corestandards.org/

Digital Resource Charts

Title	Pages	Filename
Parent Letters		
Reading Widely English	41	readingwidelye.pdf
Reading Widely Spanish	42	readingwidelys.pdf
Reading Critically English	61	readingcriticallye.pdf
Reading Critically Spanish	62	readingcriticallys.pdf
Reading Deeply English	77	readingdeeplye.pdf
Reading Deeply Spanish	78	readindeeplys.pdf
Reading Closely English	95	readingcloselye.pdf
Reading Closely Spanish	96	readingcloselys.pdf
Reading Socially English	117	readingsociallye.pdf
Reading Socially Spanish	118	readingsociallys.pdf

Title	Pages	Filename
Example Lesson Plans		
Finding a Balance of Text Types	134	balance.pdf
Introducing New Text Types	135	texttypes.pdf
Evaluating Sources	136	sources.pdf
Cross-Curricular Connections	137	connections.pdf
Preparing Students to Use Text Based Evidence	138	evidence.pdf
Preparing Students for Digital Reading Responses	139	responses.pdf
Virtual Reality Prereading Teacher Brainstorming Sheet	140	virtualreality.pdf
Passionate Readers Activity	141	passionate.pdf

Title	Pages	Filename
Example Lesson Plans		
Reading Widely Lesson	144–145	widely.pdf
Reading Critically Lesson	146–147	critically.pdf
Reading Deeply Lesson	148–149	deeply.pdf
Reading Closely Lesson	150–151	closely.pdf
Reading Socially Lesson	152–153	socially.pdf

Title	Pages	Filename
Student Reproducible Sheets		
Interest Survey 6–8	156	survey6_8.pdf
Interest Survey 3–5	157	survey3_5.pdf
Interest Survey K–2	158	surveyK_2.pdf
Reading a Blog Post	159	blog.pdf
Infographic Example	160	example_infographic.pdf
Reading an Infographic	161	reading_infographic.pdf
Creating an Infographic	162	creating_infographic.pdf
Genre Bingo	163	genre_bingo.pdf
Primary Source Analysis	164	primary.pdf
Keyword Search and Fact Finding Reflection	165	keyword.pdf
Virtual Reality Prereading	166	virtual_reality.pdf
Virtual Reality Prereading Teacher Brainstorming Sheet	167	virtual_reality_teacher.pdf
Read Aloud Planning Page	168	read_aloud.pdf
Close Reading for Multiple Perspectives	169	close_reading.pdf
Digital Anchor Charts	170	digital.pdf
Book Trailer Brainstorming Sheet	171	book_trailer_brainstorming.pdf
Book Trailer Storyboard Template	172	book_trailer_storyboard.pdf
Hashtag Reading Response	173	hashtag.pdf
Tweeting the Read Aloud	174	tweeting.pdf
Learning from Podcasts	175	podcasts.pdf

Title	Pages	Filename
Resources and Tech Tools		
All Resources and Tech Tools: Links	178–181	resources.pdf